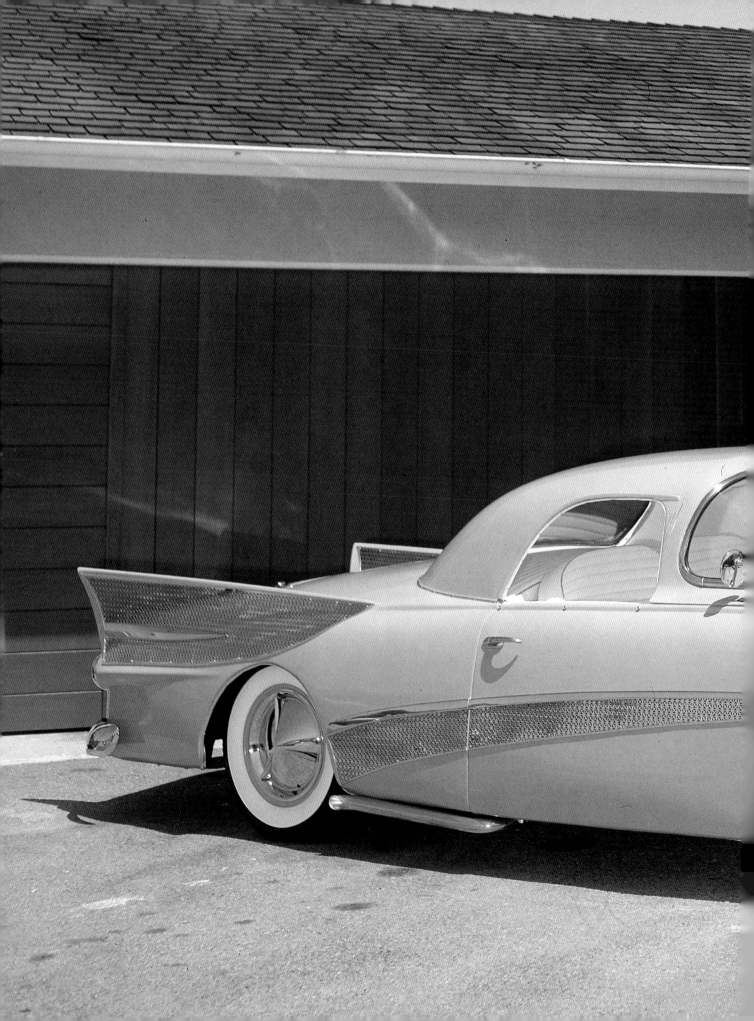

Barris

KUSTOMS
of the
1950s

George Barris and David Fetherston

Motorbooks International
Publishers & Wholesalers

First published in 1994 by Motorbooks International Publishers & Wholesalers, PO Box 2, 729 Prospect Avenue, Osceola, WI 54020 USA

Motorbooks International books are also available at discounts in bulk quantity for industrial or sales-promotional use. For details write to Special Sales Manager at the Publisher's address

Library of Congress Cataloging-in-Publication Data Available

ISBN 0-87938-943-5

On the front cover: The Barris shop built the "Emporor" in the late-fifties for Chuck Krikorian and the car won top honors at the 1960 Oakland Roadster Show. It marked the third straight year that a Barris-built entry dominated the show. *George Barris*

On the frontispiece: This is the Barris crest I discovered when I was researching my family history. Its purpose was to distinguish our cars, just as the Italian body builders Ghia, Farina, Vignale, and Touring were doing. A crest in Greece signifies a family's history, and our family had a naval tradition which included an admiral, thus the water design in the top left. The two lions signified fighting men, and the green and white stripes in the lower right are for the seaport of Argos, which was our traditional family home.

On the title page: "The Dragon," a custom 1949 Ford created by Ralph Fisher of Inglewood, California. *Barris Photo Collection*

Printed and bound in Hong Kong

Contents

Dedication: Sam Barris

*To my brother Sam Barris—
a great brother and kustomizer*

Moving down life's winding road is difficult without the help of family and friends, and it was my brother, Sam, who played an integral part in the success of our journey. We grew up in a tight-knit family which showed us that hard work and good sense would take us where we wanted.

Sam was a quiet, strong guy who could listen and direct. His eye for detail and craftsmanship helped us set a style for the "kustoms" which came through our workshop doors. Little did he know that the hammering, welding, and bodywork he so loved to do would be recognized as automotive art within a few years of his passing in 1967.

His devotion to the art of custom cars put them on a level never seen before and helped turn a hobby into a profession. Sam won dozens of awards for his work and through our combined efforts Barris Kustoms became the best-known custom car shop in the world.

The style he hammered onto the custom scene is held in great respect and is noted with the Sam Barris Award. This was initiated by his friends Harold and Willie Bagasarian and is presented at the Sacramento Autorama every year by Sam's son Johnny for "Best Kustom."

Acknowledgments

I would like to recognize contributions made by the Barris families:

George Barris Family: Shirley, Brett, JoJi, Jahon, Helen, Cassandra, Nicko, Pierre, and Greg.

Sam Barris Family: Joyce, Johnny, Pam, Brandi, Sam Jr., Barry, Katrina, Debbie, and Glen.

I would also like to list my appreciation to the great Kustomizers and the Show Promoters of the '50s:

Builders: Alexander Brothers, Joe Bailon, Andy Brizio, Carl Casper, Bill Cushenberry, Dick Dean, Jack Hageman, Bill Hines, Tommy the Greek, Dean Jefferies, Darryl Starbird, Don Tognotti, Joe Wilhelm, Gene Winfield, Don Bell, Kent Fuller, Bob McNulty, Dean Moon, Gil Ayala, Bill De Carr, Hershel "Junior" Conway, Von Dutch, and Larry Watson.

Promoters: Harold and Willie Bagdasarian, Robert and Margie Petersen, Robert Larivee Sr. & Jr., Darryl and Donna Starbird, Don and Diane Tognotti, Al and Mary Slonaker, Blackie Gejian, Ron Ail, Paul and Gene Bender, Mike Homen, Harry Costa, Carl Casper, Wally and Barbara Parks, and Bill Moeller.

Magazines and books: *Honk, Rod & Custom, Popular Hot Rodding, Car Craft, Motor Life, Motor Trend, Hot Rod, Custom Cars,* and *Trend Books.*

—*George Barris*

As a smooth-skinned kid of 12, I absorbed the customs I saw in magazines I'd snitched from my brother's friend. At the time he was attempting to customize his French Simca in a single-stall garage a few doors from my childhood home in Canberra, Australia. I could feel the passion in these cars and even though Norm's Simca didn't quite turn out looking like one of those California customs, it was quite a piece with its frenched headlights and taillights, custom grille, shaved body, and trick paint.

There was a name that occurred frequently in those days in *Car Craft* and *Hop Up* magazines: Barris. Through the subsequent years I continued to read everything I could find about the Barris brothers and their extraordinary accomplishments.

Today, thirty-five years later, I am delighted to have the opportunity to assemble this photo biography on George and Sam encapsulating their wide-reaching influence as the masters of "kustom car design" in the '50s. (I've also been able to ask George all those fascinating questions hanging around since my teenage years such as: "George, where'd you get your ideas for the design of the Golden Sahara? What kind of a person was Bob Hirohata? How did you and Sam split up the work?")

My friend Greg Williams' story is typical of how the Barris Brothers influenced other people's lives. "In 1958, when I was 13 and living in Indiana, I'd read the entire contents of those small custom magazines. 'Told my father I was leaving school to hitchhike to California and work for Mr. George Barris—I was going to work in his shop and sleep on the floor. I was going to learn from George everything about building great custom cars. My father, however, managed to keep me in school, but today I really am building those custom cars of my dreams."

As I've discovered while researching the material for this book, there were many other young men with those same dreams. One in particular, Hershel Conway, known today as "Junior," read of the Barris brothers back in Kentucky. After his family moved to Los Angeles he made his way to the Barris shop looking for help with a custom project he was finishing up with his brother. Wasn't the Barris shop, after all, the obvious place to go for custom work? George realized that the young lad had great talent from the pieces he wanted painted and offered him a part-time job. Today "Junior" is recognized as the best car painter in the world and as famous as his guru.

Kids like us loyally bent our heads and read every month about George and Sam, the Kings of Kustomizing, anointed by their masses of followers who dedicated themselves to the Barris brothers' royal passion for kustom perfection.

This book allows us to look over George and Sam's shoulders into the fifties at the cars they created and view George's historic photography of the extraordinary passage of custom cars and builders that he found across America as he worked on magazine stories on the custom lifestyle.

Thanks must go first to George for allowing this project to happen. To Greg Sharp—for being my "editorial angel," helping to factualize and fill in the blanks. To the production staff at Fetherston Publishing—Gloria Fetherston and Nanette Simmons for editorial help; to Hershel "Junior" Conway, Larry Watson, Bud Millard, Frank Livingston, Greg Williams, and Ed Roth for recalling their early years of custom cars.

—David Fetherston

Carol Lewis's 1956 Chevy was built at the shop. It was the only car that escaped the Lynwood fire. Dean Jeffries was across the street eating when the fire broke out. He raced back and saved this car before the fire took over. Barris Photo Collection

The Barris Kustom Story

By the stars or by our genes, each of us follows a path through life which we hope will evolve into a passion. So it was for the Barris brothers born in Chicago in the mid-twenties. At an early age they lost both parents, but loving relatives took them in and brought them up as their own.

In 1928, with life looking a little more rosy in California, the family moved to Roseville, just outside Sacramento, where they bought a restaurant and the boys helped out. Sam and George excelled at school and were particularly active in drawing, drama, and music.

In his free time George pursued his passion for building scratch-built models aircraft, not the plastic kits we know today. Before his tenth birthday his craftsmanship and skill had evolved from planes into model cars and led to model competitions at the local Woolworth store, where he won prizes for construction and design.

The family business flourished and expanded to include a hotel and the restaurant in Roseville. Both boys enrolled in a drama school which taught music, dance, and drama, and by age 10 they were regular troopers, performing and playing music on stage all around the Sacramento area.

Within a couple of years, as a bonus for working in the restaurant, they were given a car by their parents—a 1925 Buick sedan in need of some repair. This Buick became the first "Barris Brothers custom car."

The old Buick needed a lot of attention and their creative urges to make it different took hold. They straightened up the body and interior, adding bolt-on accessories before George hand-painted the car in orange with blue stripes. It apparently looked quite snappy as

From the earliest times Sam and I enjoyed show business. We performed on stage in Sacramento regularly, singing, dancing, or playing instruments. We did pretty well, I recall. Sam's on the right, I'm on the left.

We were both into track sports. I ran the hurdles, but Sam was the star, running the 440 at San Juan High in Roseville. This photo of me was taken about 1937.

This 1936 Plymouth was one of our first commercial customs. The owner had seen my custom 1936 Ford, so he brought his Plymouth from Oakland to Roseville to have work done on the car. Sam and I modified the nose with a Nash grille, fitted 1940 Oldsmobile bumpers, tear drop skirts, and baldy hubcaps. It was painted powder blue and finely trimmed with a white Hall upholstery top.

they promptly sold it to an eager buyer in order to purchase a 1929 Model A.

The Model A was "customized" with a slew of accessories from the local hardware store including aerials, lights, Auburn exhaust pipes coming though the side panels, and a mass of hood ornaments.

The brothers' interest in cars intensified during their teenage years as they discovered "the black art" of bodywork by hanging out after school at local bodyshops, including Brown's and Bertolucci's in Sacramento.

Around this time the boys were fortunate to meet Harry Westergard—a body man generous enough to give George and Sam his time and some of his knowledge. Harry was a metal craftsman, not just a body and fender man. His true love was custom car building, which he did with a fine sense of line and proportion.

My first hot rod was this fenderless 1932. It used the backglass from a sedan for a windshield.

When Sam came out of the service in 1945 he disembarked right into Los Angeles. I'd been running my own shop for about a year, so Sam and I combined our forces into the shop in Bell. We found this one a little later at 7674 Compton Avenue in Los Angeles. You can see my 1929 roadster, which I used for the speedway, dry lakes, and street racing.

I eventually pulled the fenders and lights off the 1929 roadster and went racing at Saugus Speedway. A few of us tried racing this roadster, then realized it wasn't what we wanted to do with our cars. But it was fun.

In Sacramento in 1948 all the guys turned out to see what we'd been doing down south. I'd just finished my custom 1941 Buick and they went nuts over it. I started the "Kustom" club in Sacramento which was the first time I used the "K" for Kustom. When I moved to Los Angeles I formed "Kustoms of Los Angeles," which was eventually renamed "Kustoms of America" (or KOA.)

George appreciated this special talent and immersed himself in as much information as Harry would let go. Harry showed him how to hand-panel body work, fabricate from sheet metal, and create new shapes out of existing ones. It was an intensive apprenticeship, and he absorbed the knowledge like a sponge soaking up water.

As George tells it: "I kept asking questions and watching. We learned to gas weld and I was allowed to try my hand at 'setting in' a license plate on a 1936 Ford. It turned out pretty good. The owner of the Ford was pleased with the way it looked. After that our real customizing began."

By this time George was 15, still fully involved in school, whereas Sam was getting ready to leave school. Both boys had taken extra classes in mechanical drawing, wood, and metal shop. George remembered: "We did anything that would teach us the skills to work on cars."

The Brothers' First Custom Job

George created his first full custom from a used 1936 Ford convertible before he graduated from high school. The combination of the newly learned metalwork skills and the urge to be different had him reworking the grille and installing Pontiac hood side panels, De Soto bumpers, and custom taillights. With all this done, George drove the 1936 down to Oakland and had Hall Upholstery install a Carson-style top.

The door and trunk handles were shaved and replaced with push buttons, the license plate was frenched, and skirts were added. "It was a super car for its time, especially when you consider there was nothing much being done anywhere like it in 1941."

A guy from Oakland saw what the boys had accomplished with the Ford and asked them to customize his 1936 Plymouth; Sam and George had found their first commercial customer. They modified the nose with a Nash grille, fitted 1940 Oldsmobile bumpers and teardrop skirts, and then drove the car down to Oakland, where Hall Upholstery fitted one of the Carson-style tops.

Meanwhile they were hanging out with kids who had similar automotive aspirations, and it was with this group that the first use of "k" for kustoms appeared. George formed the "Kustoms Car Club." Now in their mid-teens, both

Our shop was called "Barris's Custom Shop." There were a great variety of cars passing through the shop even in the early years. Here's a 1941 Chevy sitting in the driveway, which we were lightly customizing, with Nick Matranga's 1940 Mercury coupe, which we'd just started to chop, alongside it. We were also an official brake station, which helped improve the cash flow.

boys were prospects for service in World War II. George applied for both the Navy and the Army and was turned down, while Sam was called up and entered the merchant marine in 1943.

With Sam away George was left out on a limb. The brothers had worked as a team and George knew it was up to him to learn more before Sam returned. Like artistic bohemians who had gone before him, George set out on his own voyage of adventure and learning, heading south to Los Angeles where he'd heard "custom" cars were cruising the streets.

George found a group of teenage hot rodders and custom car guys to cruise with, but the

Due to the good weather much of the major work was done outside. Here you can see Sam on the left lifting the top off Jesse Lopez's 1941 Ford.

"Barris's Kustom Grilles" was one of our first product lines that gave us an identity. We were building floating grilles and installing Oldsmobile and Cadillac grilles under the Barris's Kustom Grilles name.

This custom 1940 Mercury was fitted with a 1948 Cadillac grille and was typical of a top-line street custom from around 1950.

cruising was short-lived—he mangled the front end of his 1936 convertible. Bad luck turned to good luck—he stumbled upon the Jones Brothers' bodyshop on Florence and Main in Los Angeles, where he could fix his car in exchange for working on customers' repair jobs.

The Jones brothers were well pleased with their "new employee" and quickly took note of his customizing talents. George began bringing in new clientele to the shop, young people who wanted a few extra touches done to make their cars different.

George could see his new life emerging. He had applied to go to the Art Center to learn design, but his work and skills with custom bodywork soon had him opening his own small shop in Bell, a Los Angeles suburb, in late 1944.

After Sam was discharged from the merchant marine in Los Angeles in late 1945, he joined George at the shop. George immediately took him on a tour of what was happening with custom cars and hot rods. He introduced him to the cruisers and the hot rodders who hung out at the Huntington Park Clock Drive-in, the Piccadilly off Sepulveda Boulevard, and the Circle and Hody's in Long Beach.

"We used to watch the hot rod guys street racing on the old Sepulveda Highway," George recalled. "The customs didn't race, they weren't into that, but we would turn up to watch and light up the highway with our headlights. The hot rodders would crank off down the road until some poor sucker was nailed going 100mph. The cops would show up from the other direction, lights flashing and sirens howling. You should have seen the traffic jam when that happened—everyone trying to leave at the same time!"

George and Sam pooled their resources and opened a new shop at 7674 Compton Avenue in Los Angeles. It was here that George started on his first major custom. He selected a 1941 Buick convertible, and by the time he was finished, it featured fade-away fenders and skirts, a 1941 Cadillac grille, Oldsmobile bumpers, frenched headlights, custom taillights, and the first Royal Metallic Maroon paint seen on a custom. A Carson-style top by Glen and Bob Houser finished it off.

The Buick attracted a lot of press for the new shop. It appeared on the cover of *Road and Track* and helped promote the brothers' new business. The shop was known as the "Barris's Custom Shop" and flourished immediately. Sam's natural talents for metal craftsmanship served as a perfect foil to George's desire to design, paint, manage, and promote.

We built this 1936 Ford with a Nash grille, solid side panels, teardrop skirts, and a chopped Carson-style top. We were using Bill Gaylord's shop to cover the tops. We were making the frames ourselves and had Bill cover them, but soon he started making the frames himself and doing the entire process.

Saturday afternoons the back of the Compton Ave shop became a hangout before we went to the Corona Speedway on Sundays. This was bench rac- *ing at its best. The kids would come by with rods and customs, and it helped us create a lot more business.*

MOTOR TREND

The Magazine for a Motoring World

JULY 1951 25c

TESTING THE NEW ECONOMY CHAMP
by Griff Borgeson

The Rebuilt Engine Racket

CUSTOMIZE YOUR CAR'S INTERIOR

The boys are outside the shop on Florence Avenue in Bell, where we'd just sliced the top off a 1942 Ford. That's me on the right in the baggy pants with Gene Simmons, Bill De Carr, Hector, and Bob Ruble.

We'd reworked the nose of this Ford, getting it ready for the Cadillac grille, which was fitted but not completed.

The Growth of Customizing

California in the immediate post-war years was a boom state with a massive influx of new residents from the Midwest. There was money to spend, and it was being spent mostly on two items—houses and automobiles.

Returning servicemen had yearnings for new and interesting automobiles, but with the

Although Johnny Zaro's 1941 Ford convertible appeared on the cover of the July 1951 Motor Trend, we'd built it almost three years earlier. It was one of our most popular early customs with its full fade-away fenders, chopped top, and radical channel job.

cost and scarcity of new vehicles in this post-war period so acute, custom cars offered an alternative to those wanting something different. In the pre-war years Darrin, Derham, and Bohmam and Schwartz had built custom body-work for high-dollar clients, but the new trend toward custom-built cars was coming from a middle-class market.

Unlike earlier custom-bodied vehicle builders, the new customizers had no marketing plans, no significant customer base, and they lacked virtually any form of advertising other than line of sight and word of mouth. However, the need to be different was emerging in the youth; they didn't want to drive "their father's Oldsmobile."

ROAD AND TRACK

Built on a 1947 BUICK chassis by Barris's Custom Shop, this sleek convertible sedan is only 4'10" high and is powered by a chromed full-race Buick engine of 225 h.p. Lowering was accomplished by channeling the frame and reducing the top by 4". Fenders were hand formed and are faired into the body without seams. Complete electrical push-button operation is provided for doors, luggage compartment lid, hood, windows, seat adjustment, radio aerial, and direction indicator. Each operation is indicated to the driver by a separate signal light on the dash. A curb "feeler" operates a buzzer and flashing light when contact is made. Upholstery is red and white leather.

MAY 1948   **25 CENTS**

My 1941 Buick convertible was on the cover of Road and Track *in March, 1948. The magazine was new, with only 30 pages, yet even then it was a great honor to be on the cover.*

Along with hot rodding, custom cars may well be one of the most significant trends to evolve from California in the past fifty years. America was in love with the automobile and the Barris brothers can be considered the California cupids who helped fuel the nation's continuing love affair with the automobile.

Sam and George worked on as much original customizing as they could find, and when they couldn't find any, they took in regular bodyshop work and general auto repair along with official brake testing.

George purchased and modified a 1929 Ford roadster to race at Saugus Speedway around 1947. This lasted a few months before he switched to dry lakes racing at Muroc. His racing, however, took a back seat as the business expanded and the opportunity to build custom cars took over the brothers' passions completely.

Other forces were also at work which promoted the custom car business—a group called Hollywood Publicity Associates was organizing

its first Hot Rod Show at the Los Angeles Armory. This show was partly produced by Robert "Pete" Petersen, founder and publisher of *Hot Rod* magazine, and sponsored by the Southern California Timing Association (S.C.T.A.) and the Russetta Timing Association.

The Barris brothers were asked to exhibit the only custom car in the show, whereupon George entered his Buick. He put up a display of photos to go along with it. The spectators' reaction was terrific and very positive; they loved the custom Buick. This was a car they'd dreamed of—and here were the men who'd built it.

Modern automotive magazines were also in their infancy. *Road and Track*, *Hot Rod*, and *Motor Trend* magazine emerged around this time. All of them were immediately attracted to and providing coverage of the custom car business.

Road and Track featured George's Buick on its cover in March 1948, and followed with more pieces on Barris "kustoms" in 1949 and 1950. In December 1951, *Motor Trend* featured Sam's Mercury in its cover.

With new magazines like *Hot Rod* and *Motor Trend* just springing to life, George saw an opportunity for further promotion and income and began photographing automobiles professionally.

This certainly helped the business to flourish, and the brothers quickly outgrew the tiny Bell shop. They moved to Compton Avenue for about two years and then into a larger shop in Lynwood, which became their base of operations for the rest of the decade.

Around this time George took a trip to Europe with his mother to see the relatives in Greece. Sam had been asked to go also but decided to stay home. The journey took George through England, France, Germany, and Italy, and then to Greece. It was an eye-opener for young George, travelling through another world of automobiles, one which few in California had experienced. He saw more possibilities than he previously could have imagined, and in later years he used these ideas to build his cars.

Upon returning to California, George's keen sense of promotion saw a further opportunity to expand his viewing audience. His sense of style and design, which was already evident through his photography, gained increasing exposure as he began writing for the magazines. Soon he was not only running Barris's Kustom Shop, but was also working intensely as a journalist and photographer for hot rod and custom magazines.

This put him in an exceptional position. It gave the Barris brothers the opportunity to promote their own cars and also an outlet to boost business by demonstrating techniques through how-to articles in magazine stories.

The Hirohata Merc

At the Lynwood shop the Barris grille treatments using grilles from 1948 Oldsmobiles and 1948 and 1949 Cadillacs became a custom favorite. With the evolution of the 1949 Mercury the "floating grille" concept evolved. This prominent Barris feature is still used and enjoyed by builders today. Cadillac, Chevy, and Pontiac grilles were also modified and the first custom-made tube grilles appeared.

In 1949 Sam bought a new two-door Mercury which would spawn a whole new gender of "bathtub" Mercury customs. Sam knew the Mercury would make a great custom, and one night he started cutting it up, which was a brave move at the time. Sam had figured it all out in his head, but visitors who witnessed the cutting were shocked. However as he began to re-form the body of a brand new car, they began returning with their own Mercurys, which they wanted chopped, too.

Around this time the shop was working on Louis Bettancourt's 1949 Mercury. It had been chopped by the Ayala brothers and arrived at the Barris shop to be painted in Deep Burgundy Wine and trimmed out.

Among the regular visitors to the shop was Bob Hirohata, a young Japanese-American who

Like many custom projects in the early fifties we sometimes only did a piece of the project—the owner and other shops did other areas. Louis Bettancourt's 1949 Mercury was a project handled first by the Ayala Brothers' shop, which chopped it and did a lot of bodywork, including a full fade-away fender job. We finished the car installing the grille and headlights and then painted it. (It recently won a place in the Rod and Custom *"Top 20 Rods and Customs of All Time" list.)*

lived in Arcadia. He owned a chopped 1949 Chevy, but so admired Sam's style that he purchased a low-mileage 1951 Mercury and handed it over to Sam for a full custom job. Having now worked on several new Mercurys, Sam knew precisely how to get the roof, the trunk, and the glass blended into a beautiful form.

The Mercury apparently sat around the shop for a while, but once Sam turned his hand to the project it was out the door in less than forty days. Hirohata's only instructions had apparently been to "chop it and convert it to hard-top styling." Using a few more tricks, Sam finished Hirohata's car off so it could be shown at the 1952 Motorama. It turned out to be the sensation of the show.

The Mercury's chop was perfect, the color scheme sophisticated, and the hardtop side window treatment gave the new car a startlingly clean look. George had used the same hardtop look on Nick Matranga's 1940 Mercury Coupe. This had involved removing the window frames and the "B" pillar and replacing it all with side glass, set into custom-made chromed window frames.

It was an intense time for new customs at the shop. George and Sam maintained a staff on salary, including John and Ralph Manok. They also employed a number of part-timers, including "Jocko" Johnson and Frank Sonzogni, a Lynwood policeman. In 1954 another part-time employee was taken on, Hershel "Junior"

We did this 1941 Ford for Jesse Lopez in the late forties. We chopped it about 4in, shaved most of the trim and the drip molding, frenched the headlights, added skirts, hand-formed taillights into the bumper guards, and added a 1948 Cadillac grille and 1946 Ford bumpers. We painted it Forest Metallic Green, which was most unusual for the time. Jesse lowered it and fitted Cadillac hubcaps and white wall tires.

Conway. Junior had come into the shop with some parts he wanted painted. George saw the pieces and was impressed by their craftsmanship; he offered Junior a job.

George changed the shop staff make-up in the mid-fifties. He retained only a couple of body and paint guys, including Junior, who was now a full-time employee, and began renting out space to pinstripers, painters, and upholsters. This afforded the brothers the opportunity to get their projects completed and still oversee the work to their satisfaction.

George formed "Kustoms of Los Angeles," which was initially restricted to Barris customers and later became "Kustoms of America." The group grew out of weekend "kustom runs," which George helped put together, to popular resorts like Balboa Island and Newport. "We'd all troop down to one of these places over Easter and have a ball for the weekend, dancing, partying, and showing off the cars. It became so popular, people used to come down to Newport every year just to see the cars."

Birth of the 'Golden Sahara'

The "Golden Sahara" came along about this time. George was returning from Northern California in his new 1953 Lincoln Capri, towing Dan Landon's 1949 Chevy, which had blown its engine on a trip north. Heading south on the Ridge Route out of Bakersfield, George collided with a hay truck, destroying the Lincoln.

This wild 1941 Ford belonged to Joe Urritta from Fresno. Called the "Four Foot Ford" in Rod and Custom, virtually every piece of the metal on the car was altered because of its sectioned body. After it was sectioned we shaved everything, frenched the headlights, and added an Oldsmobile grille. The total bill for this car came to about $3,600, *which was quite a sum in those days. It also featured a Carson-style removable top, which was built by Marian Cattles in Sacramento. It was another of our Motor Trend cover cars and was painted in dark green at first. Then a couple of years later we repainted it in maroon.*

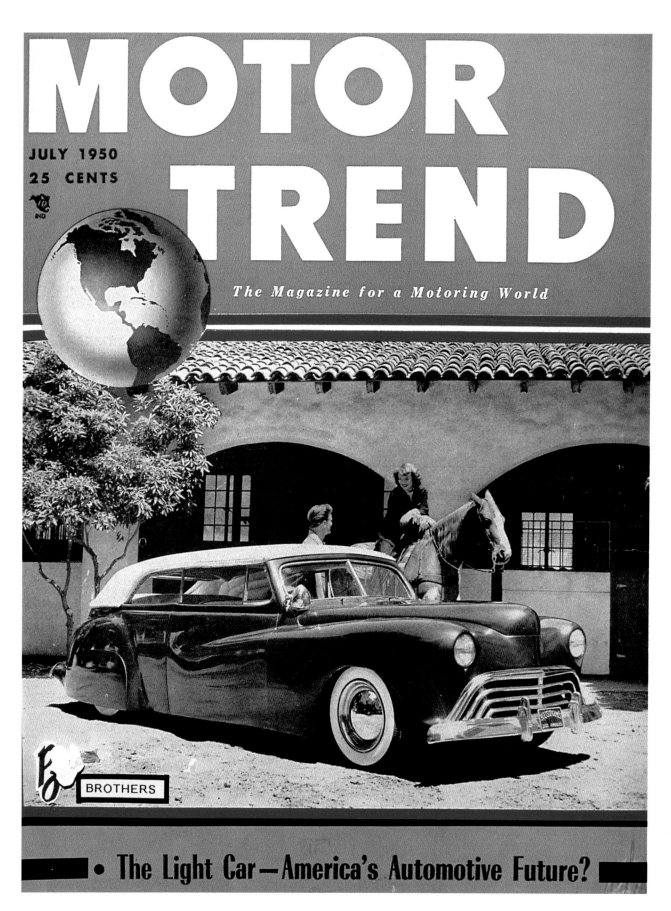

MOTOR TREND

JULY 1950
25 CENTS

The Magazine for a Motoring World

BROTHERS

• The Light Car—America's Automotive Future?

Nick Matranga's coupe was a major undertaking. We had it in the shop for over a year getting the top chop right so the body fell away gracefully. We did an amazing amount of work to this car with Sam perfecting not only his chop for this body but detailing it with his "hardtop" framed side windows, molded paneling, and a complete shave. When we chopped it we raised the windshield space into the roof line which gave it an even smoother look. We painted it in Royal Maroon with a gold iridescent finish, which produced a rich blood color. We sold this car for Nick a couple of years later while he was still in the service, fighting in Korea. It made the Rod and Custom "Top 20 Rods and Customs of All Time" list.

The accident peeled the top off the car and left George lying on the floor, but he was virtually uninjured. He shipped the Lincoln's remains back to the shop and then realized that an opportunity had been presented to him—he would take the remains of the Lincoln and create a completely original design. He sold the idea to Jim Street from Dayton, Ohio, and started creating the body. It became a sensation when it was introduced in 1955.

Joe Urritta's "Four Foot Ford" was featured on the cover of Motor Trend in July, 1950. It was one of the most extensive custom conversions done at the shop in the early years, with a full section job, shaved body, Oldsmobile grille, and dark green paintwork.

The Golden Sahara was a pivotal car for the customizing business. Detroit's auto makers began to notice that their own styling was being upstaged "by a bunch of guys in California." Many of the shapes and themes which were used on the Golden Sahara were seen later on models from Detroit, including the Lincoln Futura Dream Car, which George turned into the "Batmobile" in the early sixties

Chuck Jordan, then a young designer with Cadillac, arrived at the shop to inquire about the paint colors they were using. George mixed some Kandy Kolors for him and explained that his paint processes could not be duplicated on a production line. Perhaps, however, they could. Interestingly, we can now look back at the color changes on Cadillacs as they began to follow the custom color trends.

Other custom touches coming out of Detroit at that time included Cadillac's expanded use of bumper bullets, Lincoln's scooped rear fender treatment in 1957, and Chrysler's use of the continental wheel impression in the trunk lids of 1957-1958 Imperials and the 1960 Valiants. The roots of these styling touches can be traced to the California custom scene—and the Barris shop in Lynwood was a beehive of activity. Work continued around the clock, which, George recalls, did not endear them to the neighbors. "We had guys coming and going at all hours with most of them arriving at high speed and leaving in the same fashion."

It was here that the art of modern custom cars emerged. The volume of cars coming through the shop allowed the brothers an op-

portunity to build award-winning custom cars. They served a solid apprenticeship customizing cars of the same model repeatedly, getting closer to perfection with each job. Eventually they matched craftsmanship with speed that came from practical experience.

Their innovative work included two stunning Sedanca de Villes during these years. They were not show cars but were, rather, customs built for everyday use. Both cars featured a chopped landau top sectioned in the upper half, which then dropped down between the fenders, allowing the retention of the original fender lines. The rear end was also customized to create a new look with a counter-sunk continental spare.

Chopping, sectioning, channeling, and lowering became routine procedures at the Barris

The new 1949 Mercurys arrived. Sam knew immediately that this was going to be "the" car to customize. He went out and bought one. He used it every day, and then one night when he had figured it out, he started cutting. By the time he was finished he had created the classic Mercury custom. It was chopped and then revised with all the right touches, including frenched headlights, fade-away *fender lines, and no drip moldings. Also popular at the time were very small taillights that could be hidden in the body and bumper guards. This got us into some hassles with the police, but we could usually talk them out of it. With this car Sam pioneered the chopped Mercury look which became so popular in the fifties. (Sam's Mercury is now owned by Tommy Lee in New Jersey and is being restored.)*

24

Barris Kustoms had a stand on the north wall at many of Petersen Motorama shows at the Pan-Pacific Auditorium in Los Angeles. We would put on a display of six or eight customs at this show and promote Kustoms of America. It became a great place to unveil new customs, including the Golden Sahara.

shop. Other techniques were also perfected, including the V-butted windshield and Kandy Kolored paintwork. Customers brought cars in from as far away as New Jersey and Ohio.

The Brothers 'Go Hollywood'

Enter Hollywood. Folks at the movie studios had taken note of the flamboyant Barris Kustoms on the streets of their city and came knocking at the door wanting cars for their films. MGM asked the brothers to build a pair of chopped custom 1948 Chevrolets for a street racing scene in a movie called *High School Confidential.*

One of the cars was to be rolled during the race. As it turned out, the chopped and lowered 1948 coupe couldn't be rolled, so the scene was faked by dropping the car from a crane and hurling wheels and body pieces through the air to create the appearance of an accident.

The success of their initial movie car venture spurred George to seek part of his business in Hollywood. As the past forty years have shown, this association has been a long and fascinating trip with dozens of movie credits including the Barris name.

George's connections with Hollywood continued as he became a talent agent for other owners' and builders' hot rods and customs. He made sure that they were the correct style and color, and that they were at the right movie location on time. These cars included a roadster for the TV series "Window on Main Street," a chopped 1934 coupe owned by Jim Griepsma for the TV show "Life of Riley," and a traditional 1929 roadster which featured in a "Dragnet" episode called "The Big Rod." George formed

25

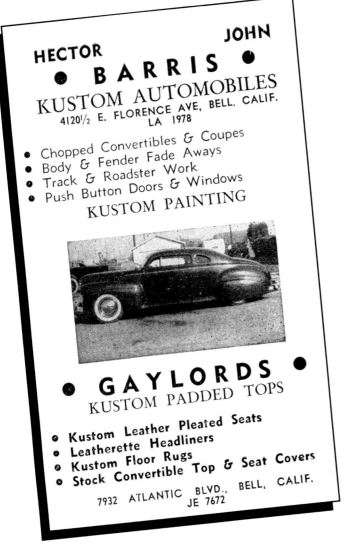
customs they'd been building. These ideas did, however, relate to the special custom cars sought in Hollywood, and thus the shop began customizing for the likes of stars such as Liberace, Jayne Mansfield, and George Raft.

George's work with the magazines expanded and even Sam turned out a few stories for *Rod and Custom*. Spence Murray's "*Rod and Custom* Dream Truck" came and went from the shop for a while as George and Sam reworked the body with new headlights, front and rear grilles, a roof scoop, and new paintwork.

The Shop Fire

Then, tragedy struck. A fire on December 7, 1957, gutted the Lynwood shop and put a brake on things for a while. The fire started on a rainy night when the power lines at the back of the shop bounced off each other and sent a heavy shower of sparks down on the roof of the shop. The fire started out in the back of the shop and the only way to get to it was from L.A. county property. Unfortunately, the Lynwood Fire Department did not have authorization to cross the boundary and they waited 40 minutes for the L.A. Fire Department to arrive and hose the fire down from the rear.

Fourteen cars were destroyed in the fire including boxing champion Archie Moore's magnesium-bodied Jaguar, actress Jayne Mansfield's Jaguar roadster, and the Sarabian brothers' "Wild Kat" Ford F-100 pickup. The fire stopped just before reaching Richard Peters's "Ala Kart."

Dean "Jeff" Jeffries was having dinner across the street at the time and raised the

associations with many of Hollywood's entertainers through this work.

Although George's earlier trip to Europe had given him an infusion of customizing ideas, most of them did not apply to the traditional

Left
Jack Stewart's 1941 Ford coupe. This car was started by the Ayala Brothers and brought over to us to finish. It had been chopped and sectioned so the section ran under the fade-away fenders. The body creases were also removed and a 1949 Cadillac grille was installed along with a new flat hood. I recall it was painted in a bronze metallic. It is seen here at a show before it was finished, with the windows blocked out as it didn't have the interior completed. (The Ford is now restored and owned by Bob Drake in Indiana.)

Opposite page
Sam's Mercury was featured on the cover of Motor Trend. This was shot when a group of us headed into the San Bernardino mountains. We built a snowman for the photo, and a couple of friends, Carol Brewer and Dale Marshall, were models.

MOTOR TREND

The Magazine for a Motoring World

DECEMBER 1951 25c

YOUR *FLYING CAR* IS HERE TODAY

Page 15

SAM BARRIS

alarm. He rescued one car as the place went up.

George's insurance company never paid off. They claimed the fire was "an act of God." This bad news heavily affected George, but the owner of the building also had insurance which *did* cover "an act of God." The shop was quickly rebuilt. One section of it had not been damaged, so work proceeded in that area while the rest of the shop was being repaired.

Shirley Nahas, George's future wife, now became a strong nurturing partner in George's life as Sam had already left the business. She redecorated the shop, "Zolatone" painting the office and adding a few feminine touches to a world of hard parts.

Sam's chopped 1949 Mercury coupe was the cover car of Motor Trend *in December 1951. Sam pondered how he would chop the Mercury, and it became a part-time project during the next four months.*

Sam had decided even before the fire to return to Sacramento to accept employment as an accident investigator for an insurance company. The brothers had split up in an amicable fashion, but George missed the company of a brother he'd worked and played with for thirty years.

Yet Sam continued some customizing in Sacramento, functioning as the Northern California Division of Barris Kustoms, and he added one more major custom to his list of achievements. Known as the "El Capitola," it was a heavily customized 1957 Chevy 210 coupe built for Don Fletcher. Sam did the metal work, including a complete new front end and 1957 Lincoln tailfins. It was then shipped to George for painting and finishing in Lynwood. Completed in 1960, "El Capitola" was the last major project worked on by both George and Sam.

Gene Simmons became general manager of the Lynwood shop and continued Sam's good work. George Barris began appearing on

This 1947 Buick was a super car we built for custom furniture manufacturer Ben Mario and his wife Helen. We used one of our neatest tricks, which was to customize it by changing the bodywork with a 1948 Cadillac grille and rear fenders. We nosed and decked the hood, frenched the headlights, and lowered the suspension 6in. It was then finished in a beautiful purple-tone paint with a gray and white interior. (Ben still has the car.)

a weekly TV show talking about customs and hot rods and began promoting his own hot rod and custom car shows in Southern California.

His work at the shop changed from building cars to designing them, doing promotion, and, of course, management. He traveled across America with his promotional "Kopper Kart," a heavily customized six-cylinder Chevy pickup built at the Lynwood shop. George was also still filling unique niche as a photographer and journalist covering the car shows for *Rod and Custom* and *Hot Rod* magazines. Throughout the fifties George visited custom builders across the country. He toured the Alexander Brothers' shop in Detroit and was the first to put out the news in West Coast magazines on these creative guys.

The Lynwood shop now had customs com-

ing in for a second and a third re-work. The "Grecian," a 1948 Studebaker four-door sedan, went through two complete custom make overs. It was first completed in 1952, then re-

Opposite page
Art and Lloyd Chrisman's 1930 Model A Bonneville coupe used a pair of 1940 Ford hoods to form a streamlined nose along with its chopped top. Back in 1954 when this shot was taken, the coupe had just run 195mph at Bonneville. It later ran over 200mph. I purchased the car in the early sixties and renamed it the "XMSC 210" for the Dwayne Hickman "Dobie Gillis" TV show. We set it up like a street racer for the show rather than a lakes car. I had John Geraghty install a fully chromed, blown Oldsmobile engine and chromed suspension, and we added gull-wing doors so the car could be used for filming. Barris Photo Collection

done in dynamic yellow and green in 1960 and was renamed the "Modern Grecian."

Every make and model of car or truck was tackled in the shop, whether it was steel or fiberglass. Coupes, trucks, and sedans all went under the hammer, including Cadillacs, Buicks, Oldsmobiles, Studebakers, Jaguars, Fords, and Lincolns. Even Ferraris underwent the "kustom" treatment.

The work going through the shop wasn't just building complete customs. There was a steady flow of minor custom bodywork, frenching, and paint being turned out on a regular basis, too.

Around 1957 Kandy Apple paint became very popular, but as many painters found out, it was difficult to apply correctly. "Junior," who

had been the prep boy at the shop for several years, now worked very closely with George applying these trick colors. Initially, George had let Junior do only the preparation and base colors before George applied the final Kandy coats. But as the shop got busier, Junior took over the whole Kandy paint process.

"Ala Kart" was on the work agenda for 1957. It was built in the shop to George's design for Richard Peters's entry in the "America's Most Beautiful Roadster" competition at the Oakland Roadster Show. It won this prestigious award in 1958 and 1959, the show's first back-to-back winner.

Bill Hines arrived in 1958 from Michigan with his custom 1950 Ford, "The Bat." Bill worked on several Thunderbird projects at the shop includ-

We built this streamliner body in 1953 for Chet Herbert, whom you can see in the wheelchair near the rear of the car. It was originally fitted with a four-cylinder two-stroke Weir engine that had been designed for a 1932 Indy 500 racer. Its low profile was perfect for a streamliner, but the engine was destroyed on the dyno only a short time before it was due to go to the salt. Sam had to blister out the body to suit a Hemi engine instead, which they

quickly installed. It was all done with hammers, leather bags, and bucks. We went to Bonneville with the car, where I recall it ran close to 235mph. There'd been no time to put Dzus fasteners into the alloy body, so it was held together with sheet metal screws. By the end of the first pass all the screws had vibrated loose, so we had to re-screw the removable body sections before the car could make its return pass.

Sam's next car after his Mercury was this 1950 Buick sedanette. Sam got it cheap after it had been in a garage fire. This car came out beautifully. The top chop was difficult, as the trunk lid needed a V-section removed so he could lay down the shape of the new top into the bodywork. The top took two to three months to get done, but the results were great. Sam also frenched in the oval Buick headlights and installed a floating Oldsmobile grille and Cadillac hubcaps. Gaylord's did the interior, and the Golden Maroon Bronze Buick ended up on magazine covers. (It has been restored and is owned by Barris collector, Kurt McCormick, in St. Louis.)

ing the 1958 for Shirley Barris, Larry Watson's 1958, and the 1957 "Xtura" belonging to Mitch Nagao. Junior worked alongside Bill Hines on these projects absorbing everything Bill could teach about body and painting techniques while striving to achieve perfect paint.

Another of the shop's customs to hit the front page was Bill Carr's "Aztec." It was featured as the lead photo with the 1958 *Motor Trend* story, "The Man who Changed the Face of Detroit." The story covered how custom cars and Barris had changed—for the better—the look of Detroit production cars.

The "Aztec" was done by Bill with the help of Bill Ortega and Barris Kustoms over a couple of years. It featured 1957 Mercury Turnpike headlights which had been semi-tunneled, and taillights which were hand-formed in red Lucite by Bob Hirohata.

In 1959 George appeared in an annual *Car Craft* magazine feature called "Custom Forecast." George predicted correctly that 1959 would be the year of the Integrated Custom and that "we will see the introduction of 'plastic' customizing this year, a new low cost, easy to replace technique." In the article he also pre-

Bill De Carr did custom work for us at the shop and built this super 1941 Mercury custom during that time. He built up this Ford at the shop with a 6in chop to the roof and a 5in channel, frenched headlights, shaved trim, and drip molding, Oldsmobile grille, Chevy bumpers, and full fade-away fenders. As I recall, it was finished in a dark green. (Bill still does fabulous metal work.)

dicted that square headlights would be a feature of the future and that he was looking for a manufacturer to make them.

By 1959 the custom business was at its peak, but times were changing. The interest in traditional customs was waning and high performance was taking over the shows and the marketplace. At the Barris shop, this did not go unnoticed, and George began looking around for a shop closer to Hollywood.

In the late fifties George and Revell, the model kit maker, signed a licensing agreement and Revell started making plastic kits of a 1956 Buick Barris custom. AMT immediately joined the fray and offered George a new deal to do the Ala Kart. It came out as the "Ala Kart 2-in-1 Kustomizing Kit," which quickly evolved into the 3-in-1 series of kits. The sales of these kits took off at an amazing rate and within eighteen months plastic car model kits were the biggest selling toys on the toy market.

The idea was emulated immediately by oth-

"Snooky" Janich's 1941 Ford was a business coupe with a short roof. This meant his Ford needed a different chop compared to regular 1941 Ford coupes. The body paneling had been molded in and the trim *was shaved. We took the creases out of the fenders on this one. It featured a 1946 Chevy grille which had been shortened to fit.*

er plastic kit manufacturers. These custom kits gave many hours of pleasure to thousands of young kids and encouraged them to learn about automobiles and customs.

George was on a roll for the end of the fifties. He pulled off yet another triumph, accomplishing the seemingly impossible task of a third straight win at Oakland when Chuck Krikorian's "Emperor" was named "America's Most Beautiful Roadster" in 1960. The custom award that year went to El Capitola, making it a double header for George and a great final win for Sam.

Original kustoms and hot rods continued to roll off George's drawing board, and they were built and decorated by some of the best fabricators and craftsmen in the business. Over the years this pool of talent has included Bill Hines, Lloyd Bakan, Dick Dean, Dean Jeffries, Von Dutch, Larry Watson, Hershel "Junior" Conway, John and Ralph Manok, Bill De Carr, Richard Korkes, Frank Sonzogni, "Jocko" Johnson, Lyle Lake, Curley Hurlbert, "Gordo," and for a brief time, magazine publisher Tom McMullen. Many of them went on to do their own notable work in and around custom cars, hot rods, and the movie business.

But George wasn't just a rock running the business. He married Shirley in 1958 and gave her a Cadillac custom as a wedding present. She became a positive force in his life, assisting him with his story ideas and interior design, helping the business grow strong, and even posing with cars for photos. In the early sixties she and George had two children, JoJi and Brett, and their family roots still hold tight.

As the sixties began, George shifted gears and bought a new shop on Riverside Drive in North Hollywood. He moved in by the end of 1961.

Kustom car history began emerging through the portal of a new decade. Barris hot rods won yet another two "America's Most Beautiful Roadster" awards at Oakland and George continued designing and building cars like the "Surf Woody" and the "Twister T." But their stories are from the new decade and we'll keep them for another book . . .

Bob Hirohata is leaning on his Hirohata Mercury (far right), which we had repainted just before it appeared in the film Running Wild. *Its new colors were Seafoam Green and Organic Green. Bob had just collected yet another trophy at the Renegades Show in Long Beach. (The Hirohata Mercury is now being restored and will be seen again in 1995.)*

Bob Hirohata had seen Sam's Mercury and wanted one just like it. Sam chopped the top, V-butted the glass, and frenched the headlights. All the factory trim was shaved and 1952-1953 Buick side trims were fitted. Sam eliminated the doorpost and re-framed the windows just as he had with Matranga's Mercury. Bob is seen here beside the Mercury with a trophy from the South Gate High School show. At this stage of its life the Hirohata car was painted Seafoam Green with Organic Green side panels.

Opposite page
This sectioned 1937 Ford truck was built by the Valley Custom Shop in Burbank for Tommy Jamieson. It was one of the best-looking custom pickups of its time and is still a stand-out design. The cab was sectioned 5in while the bed was shortened about a foot. They also slanted back the grille shell, which gave it a much smoother line. Barris Photo Collection

There were several shops doing custom work in the Los Angeles area. We were busy doing work ranging from simple add-ons to a full custom conversion. This 1942 Ford we built for Ann Reynolds was chopped and fitted with a 1948 Oldsmobile grille and bumper. We cleaned up the body with some shaving, molding, and new paint and interior. The bill was probably less than $2,000—we used to charge about $350 for a steel roof chop, $100–$150 for a convertible, and paint was $150–$200.

"We have a lot of trust in each other. My wife had a hospital emergency and I needed money which I didn't have. I called George to ask him what to do. He was right there instantly, sorting out the hospital charges... enough said."

—Dick Dean, Custom Car Builder

Frank Monteleone's 1941 Ford convertible was a major piece of work. It really got us some attention when we stripped off all four fenders and replaced them with fenders from a 1950 Oldsmobile. This gave the Ford a new image and created quite a few headaches for us when we tried to blend the different-shaped paneling into the Ford doors. We made a steel removable top out of a chopped roof section of a 1938 Ford sedan. The car came and went from the shop several times, but eventually we finished it. It was painted pink with a black side panel and a white roof. This was shot outside the Pan-Pacific Auditorium in Los Angeles. (Frank still owns several customs including one of my Barrister coach-built Corvettes.)

This was one of the most popular 1940 Ford chops we did; it was done for Tom Hocker from Oakland, California. It had been hot rodded for quite a while before we chopped the top, shaved the body, and molded in the fenders. We also frenched in the headlights, which was unusual for a 1940 as most custom forties used stock headlight mounts. It was finished off in Silver Blue. The coupe was later converted to quad headlights and can be seen in the movie American Graffiti.

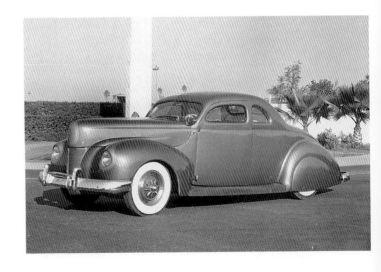

Ralph Testa's 1950 Mercury had all the tricks with shaved trim, frenched headlights, and 1949 Buick taillights that we turned sideways, along with a chopped Carson top. Sam and I turned this Mercury out in early 1952. Ralph wanted this car "low," so we lowered it 7in in the rear and 5in up front. The bill for this car was $1,750 after we'd finished it with 28 coats of Coral Blue-Purple lacquer. (This car is currently being restored in Washington state by Bill Worden.)

Chuck DeWitt owned this 1950 Ford convertible. Chuck was a USC geology student at the time. We did a lot of work on this car with its custom outer grille shell molded in with tubing and then fitted with a floating center grille bar. The grille bar was a complex piece. It used a 1952 Kaiser center bar with 1953 Mercury teeth and a pair of 1951 Henry J parking light frames that dropped under the 1950 Studebaker parking lights. It also featured molded side panels with a scoop and Mercury skirt, and custom side trim made out of Buick and Oldsmobile spears. It was painted in a rich metallic purple and proved to be very popular.

Louis Bettancourt sold his 1949 Mercury to Johnny Zupan, who had us redo some of the body detailing and apply the new metallic rust and gold paint. This photo was taken around 1956.

We did this 1949 Ford for Buster Litton. It was known as the "Panoramic Ford" and was chopped with the door posts and quarter windows removed to give the hardtop look. The front end was extended by George Cerny using 1950 Studebaker fenders and headlights. The floating grille, flared fender skirts, and the small Oldsmobile bullet taillights gave the Ford a completely new look.

41

Dan Landon's 1949 Chevrolet was a big challenge. It was one of the first cars in which we installed curved glass and chopped the top at the same time. The body was fully shaved with no drip rail. The hood was nosed and the trunk decked with frenched Kaiser taillights added to emphasize the teardrop shape of the car. It was later featured in a series of magazine articles on a cross-country road trip.

It's great to see "The Golden Sahara" being used, not stored. Here it's towing a Chris Craft Cobra powerboat. We based the Golden Sahara on my wrecked 1953 Lincoln Capri. It was built from the ground up for Jim Street with a transparent hinged top while the interior featured a TV, phones, and reel-to-reel tape player. The front end featured huge bumper bullets with mesh grillework which we ran up and under the headlight eyebrow, and the side panels were gold plated. This is the Golden Sahara in its second generation, which added more gold trim, split V-fins, and a chrome band over a bubble windshield. (Jim still drives the Sahara.) Barris Photo Collection

This is Bob Hirohata's Mercury in its first generation paintwork of Seafoam and Green with Marilyn Bordeau modeling. The "Hirohata Mercury" was unique at the time. Sam had already chopped a couple of Mercurys, but Hirohata's car used chromed side window moldings that were sculptured to give a hardtop appearance like Matranga's Mercury Coupe. The 1953 Buick Riviera side trim was blended into the rear quarter and the rear fender skirt matched the front flare. In fact, everything matched. It all had rhyme and reason. The floating grille ended with handmade plastic directional signal lenses, and the interior knobs were also handmade from laminated plastic sheets. Bob Hirohata used to make some of these for us, along with taillight lenses. Ralph Poole Photo

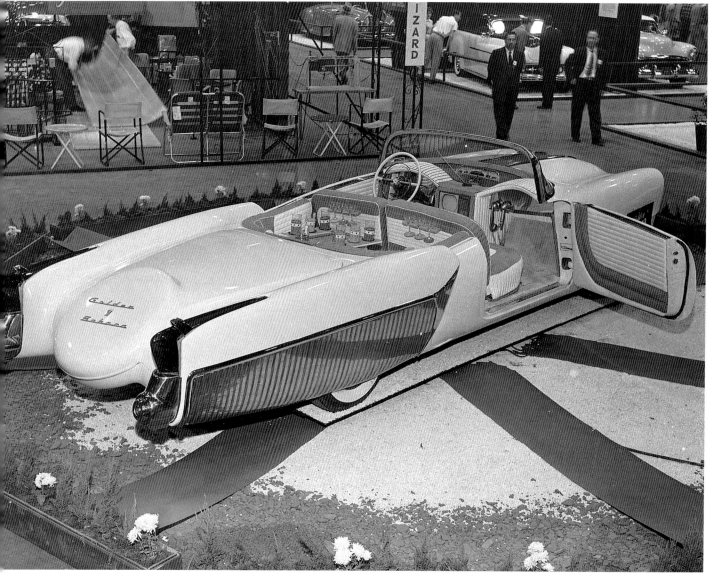

The "Golden Sahara" was our first coach-built body and our answer to Detroit's "Dream Cars." Everything was hand-built on the body. I'd just purchased a new 1953 Lincoln Capri and was heading back from Sacramento when I ran under a hay truck, crushing the front and the top. It was brought back to the shop, and my brain went berserk with possible designs. Jim Street from Dayton, Ohio, loved the design idea, so we had a buyer. Sam followed through with the body using my design.

From the early days, I was taking pictures of every-thing we did. I was shooting masses of photos for Hop Up, Hot Rod, and Rod and Custom magazines at Petersen. As I traveled with my cars to numerous shows, it was natural for me to cover those shows and shoot the pictures. I developed it into a second profession, and it got me a lot of added exposure. Here I am at Teaneck, New Jersey, in the mid-fifties with my faithful old Rolleiflex.

"The Mandarin" was a four-door 1950 Mercury Sedan we built for Bill Busch. It was nosed and decked with an oval grille shell and frenched Ford headlights. We finished it off with push-button elec- tric doors, flared full skirts, and a floating Plymouth grille. We built this car at Lynwood and painted it with Mandarin Maroon lacquer. Barris Photo Collection

Opposite page
Ralph Fisher from Inglewood, California, created a different custom with this pink and silver coupe when he chopped, sectioned, and channeled a 1949 Ford into "The Dragon." I liked this car because its character was so different with the use of chrome and fins. It didn't quite balance but created an interesting look. Barris Photo Collection

I built the "Kopper Kart" out of a six-cylinder-powered 1956 Chevy which had been partly customized with a 5 1/2in section. We then sliced in a 4in chop and did extensive bodywork on every panel with a lot of copper plating, which gave it an interesting golden look. The white and copper Naugahyde interior was installed by Gaylord's. The body rework included the pancaked hood with twin air scoops, peaked front fenders, and full-flowing rear pan. The Kopper Kart won so many trophies on its tours back East I was glad it was a truck, so I could cart them home. I sold the Kopper Kart to the Ohio owner of Porky's Drive In, and it was last seen abandoned in a field near Morrison Town, Ohio, in the early sixties. Barris Photo Collection

Jon Southwick from El Cerrito restyled this 1954
Buick convertible. The oval grille used a mass of
chrome bullets made with 1956 Buick bumper guard
centers. Other custom work included the quad
headlights and a frenched license plate mount. It
had custom rear fenders which used 1955 Chrysler
taillights, while the side trim is stock Buick. The
wheels are chrome reversed with hubcap bullets
made from 1936 Oldsmobile headlight housings.
Barris Photo Collection

I shot Ed Sloan's unusual 1953 Plymouth custom
outside the Compton Drive-in. We chopped the
top, molded in a custom grille shell, fitted a floating
grille made from a variety of Ford grille pieces,
frenched the headlights, and installed 1953 Lincoln
taillights. It also featured scooped skirts with side
trim which extended from the door into the rear
quarter. It was finished in Dark Green metallic and
Lime Mist.

65

We did this 1954 Eldorado convertible for Milton Melton, a Los Angeles supermarket executive. The top was chopped into a half top by coachbuilder Bohman and Schwartz, with sectioning done on the upper half of the body, which was then dropped down between the fender lines in a kind of Sedanca de Ville style. We also countersunk the spare into the trunk rather than have it stick out; this allowed us to keep the original fender lines without the stock fin. The Cadillac created a sensation at the 1955 International Motor Revue. (It has just been restored Kurt McCormick in St. Louis.)

Larry Ernst arrived from Toledo, Ohio, with his 1951 Chevy Bel-Air and said "give me something different." Well, Sam looked at this Chevy after doing a handful of Mercurys and figured it would take some work because of the hardtop styling. This was the first Bel-Air that was chopped that I know of, and it turned out to be quite a challenge for Sam, but he pulled it off just perfectly. The top was chopped 2 1/2in while the windshield posts were laid back 2 1/2in. Sam then dropped the rear of the roof 6in, which gave it a swooping, tapered line. The new roofline created a couple of other problems because Larry wanted a Continental spare and I couldn't talk him out of it. To hide the wheel from just sticking out the back Sam extended the fenders 12in while adding 2in to their lower edges. The windshield is a one-piece curved unit cut down from a 1951 Oldsmobile. The Bel-Air was painted in two-tone metallic purple with a light orchid top. It was in the shop for three months, but two years later we re-did this car with new paint and added some bodywork detailing. It became known as the "Bel Aire Royale." (Now restored and owned by Burns Berryman in Michigan.)

"Von Dutch" came in one afternoon to do a little pinstriping on our flamed Ford Woody wagon. It was supposed to be a simple, small striping job. He opened a bottle of wine and started striping away while we were working on other shop projects. The next thing I knew it was midnight and he wasn't finished, so I left him in the shop and went home.

When I came in the next morning, he was still striping. He'd written a story into the pinstriping about the shop and in doing so had turned a simple job into an art project that worked its way around the wagon. It was pretty wild but typical of Dutch. The next time I used him, I supervised him a lot more.

The "Cadillac LeMans" was an ex-GM show car owned by the shoe magnate Harry Karl. Harry gave the Cadillac as a gift to his actress wife Marie McDonald after we had re-sculptured some of the paneling, added gold trim, a bar behind the seat, a TV, and painted it in Silver Pearl. Most of the body was fiberglass, but the tail fins were chrome plated steel. This caused us a lot of headaches as the chrome guys kept messing them up with their grease wheels, which would leave grooves. Both Karl and Marie drove it on the street regularly, but I showed it for him.

This is Dave Bugarin's 1951 Mercury. We reworked the front end with frenched 1953 Buick headlights, V-butt glass, frenched 1954 Packard taillights, chopped top, and framed side-glass like Hirohata's car. We painted it in two tones of Organic and Blue Fog metallic.

We had a lot people working part-time in the shop, including Frank Sonzogni, who was a local Lynwood policeman. Frank built his 1950 Mercury over two years with a chopped top, flush skirts with side scoop, V-butt glass, floating 1954 DeSoto grille, and 1952 DeSoto bumpers. It was painted in dark Organic Green with a lime green side panel. Today builders leave drip moldings on, but back then they were one of the first things to come off.

This 1951 Mercury belonged to Manny Holder. Manny came from Springfield, Illinois, to have us finish this car. The Pontiac side trim matched the dip in the doors, and full side skirts were made from 1953 Ford quarter panels. The top was done at Gaylord's, and we built a custom bar grille with plastic tips for directional signals. It featured floating twin Pontiac bumpers and we painted it in two-tone metallic blue.

Freddie Rowe owned this 1951 convertible with a Carson top. It rolled on Chrysler-Kelsey-Hayes wire wheels, which were very expensive at that time. It featured Buick side spears with a scoop in the center of the curve. It also had a pair of scoops in the hood. We did the grille using stock ends with the lights, and fabricated a new center section, which we slotted and chromed. This car was used in the movie Running Wild with Mamie Van Doren. We had this car in the shop several times. (It has recently undergone a ground-up restoration back East.)

"Sam and George were like hood ornaments—way out there, ahead of the rest of us"

—Ed Roth, Artist of the Car

Opposite page
Here we have Sam's "Practical Custom" 1952 Ford that was shown on the cover of Rod and Custom in December 1955. You can see Sam's wife Joyce and his children, Johnny and Pamela, seated in the car while Louise Manok, a part-time Barris employee, is in the front seat. The Ford featured a hand-formed custom grille, hammered hood, shaved trim, padded "safety" interior, 1954 Mercury side spears, hooded headlights, Lincoln taillights, and two-tone blue and silver paintwork.

This wild-looking coupe was designed and built by Jay Everett of Gardena, California. It was one of the first hand-built cars made on an English roller in California. Jack Sutton and Dennis Power opened Auto Craft Sports Bodies to do body panels in aluminum. The coupe featured a 1953 Oldsmobile engine, tilt-forward nose, and matching grilles, front and rear. Jay wanted something different from the T-birds and Corvettes that were being built at the time. Dick Hoy bought the car unfinished from Jay and we then finished the paint and interior. It became known as the "Astra Coupe." Barris Photo Collection

DESIGNING

CONSTRUCTION

Barris
KUSTOM AUTOMOBILE
PRICE LIST

11054 ATLANTIC BLVD. LYNWOOD, CALIF.
NE 6-4432
NE 8-5256

The "Barris Kustom Automobile Price List" had photos of Sam and me on the cover along with Larry Ernst's 1951 Chevy. The price list for customizing services including a V-peaked Ford hood for $45, frenched headlights for $25 and a 25-coat Kustom paint job for $165.

Below
The movie business introduced hot rods and custom cars into their productions in the late forties. High School Confidential was one of the first to feature hot rods and customs built specifically for a movie. We built two 1948 Chevys with teardrop skirts, custom grilles, blanked outside windows, lowered suspension, and chopped tops. The movie starred Russ Tamblyn, Jan Sterling, John Barrymore, Jerry Lee Lewis, Jackie Coogan, and Mamie van Doren.

We installed a roll cage in one of the High School Confidential Chevys, but the stunt driver, Gary Laufer, couldn't roll it. It was too low. There was no way he could get it over, so they dropped it from a crane to simulate the rollover. You can see the wheel flying up in the air. Today they'd have no problem rolling the car with their modern flip-over techniques which use cannons mounted in the floor.

Here the Chevy in High School Confidential pursues a couple of roadsters just before the rollover scene.

I think I had more fun with "Kopper Kart" than with any of my earlier customs. It was so recognizable with all its bodywork and copper plating. The six-cylinder-powered 1956 Chevrolet was heavily modified with a 4in chop and a 5 1/2in section. The chop was very difficult because we couldn't cut the tempered glass. We had to lay the tips of the front glass back into a cowl recess. We drove it all over the country and spent many hours keeping up the copper plating under the hood and on the body.

I opened a new shop called Kustom Accessories in Lynwood. I rented out the space to Dean Jeffries, who did his pinstriping at the shop, and to Wilford Manuel, who did custom interior work. We also set up Lloyd Bakan in this shop to sell our Kustom Accessories.

The TV show "Window on Main Street" with Robert Young was the start of my "Twister T." It used a 1927 T body on Deuce rails with a Dodge Red Ram Hemi and Skylark wire wheels. After the TV show I rebuilt this car several times until it evolved into my Oakland Roadster Show winner in 1962.

Opposite page
One of my early TV deals was to provide a car for the "Life of Riley" TV show with William Bendix. We provided a Hemi-powered, chopped 1934 coupe with a 1932 grille shell; the car was owned by Jim Griepsma.

Hershel "Junior" Conway did his 1950 Ford coupe at the shop, and it was so low it sometimes had to be lifted over speed bumps. Junior developed his painting abilities at the shop starting with body and paint preparation and going on to painting. He began working for me part-time as a young teenager and eventually became a full-time employee. Junior built his Ford into a consistent show winner with its eyebrow headlights, bullet bumper overriders, custom side trim, trick three-tone paint, and custom scooped skirts. This was a very popular car, and I managed to get it featured in the movie Cry Out In Vengeance.

Opposite page
Sal Mammano's 1954 Buick custom was featured on the cover of Motor Life magazine in September 1956. Mammano owned the Casa Di Bella hair styling salon in Downey, California. We combined with Gaylord's to convert a rolled 1954 Buick Roadmaster Riviera into this Sedanca de Ville using a mix of Cadillac, Buick, and custom parts. It was a massive custom project, but it turned out great and got a lot of "ink." I wrote the feature story on the project for Motor Life magazine.

Buddy Alcorn's 1951 Mercury was another big hit. It featured full fade-away fenders, side scoops, and custom side trim. The front fenders were reworked with recessed frenched headlights and the rear was fitted with 1955 Plymouth taillights. It was painted in rich purple. Buddy attracted a lot of attention with the Mercury because he drove it so much. (This car has just been found again and is apparently about to be restored.)

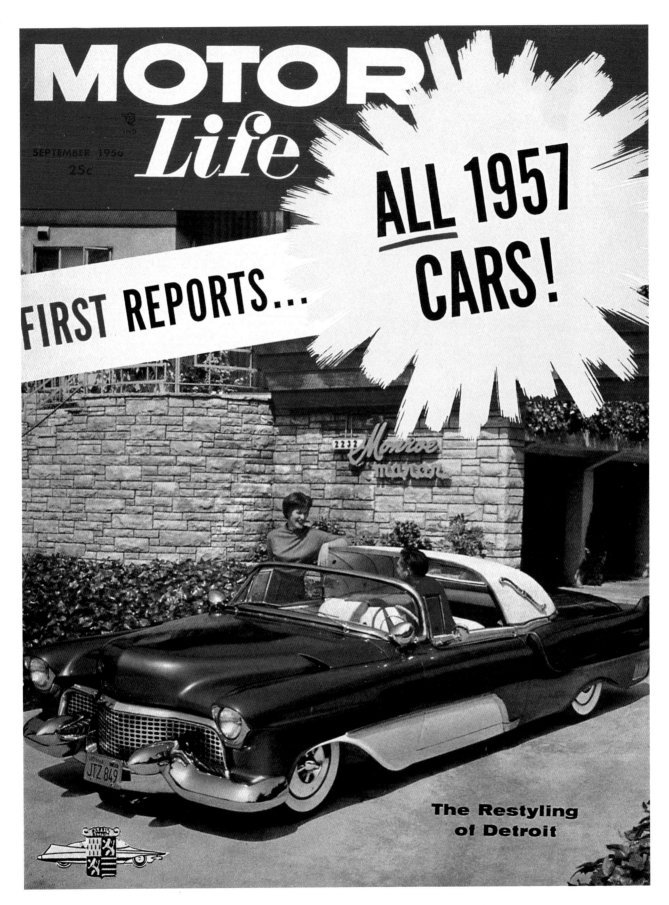

MOTOR Life

SEPTEMBER 1956
25c

FIRST REPORTS...

ALL 1957 CARS!

The Restyling
of Detroit

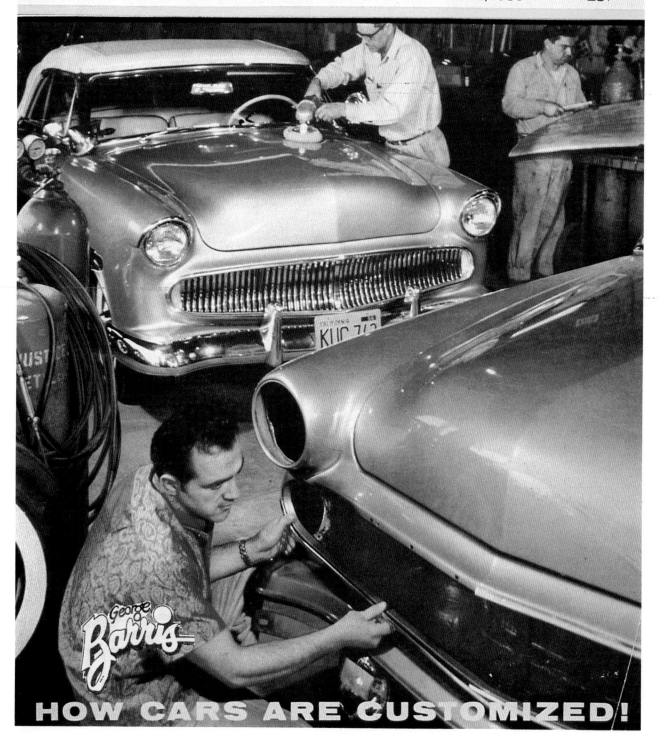

MOTOR Life

JUNE, 1956   25¢

T V
ROAD
TEST

George
Barris

HOW CARS ARE CUSTOMIZED!

My own 1956 Lincoln Mark II custom featured a white sport canvas top from Gaylord's and was lowered and painted in Bronze metallic. We got a great reaction to this car. Jayne Mansfield asked us to build one for her in brown with a mink, silk, and leather interior trim.

Bob Vincent's 1951 Mercury was built by Gene Winfield and painted in Cobalt Blue metallic with beautiful gold scallops, side impressions, and 1958 Ford side trim. It was heavily lowered and featured trick tail fins with frenched 1956 Packard lenses. It was a pretty car which Bob had titled "The Blue Blob." Barris Photo Collection

Bob Merry from San Francisco had Joe Bailon build him this radical 1954 Oldsmobile. Joe created the grille using two 1958 Plymouth front bumpers with four 1953 Dodge bumper guards at each end surrounding a Corvette grille. The quad headlights on Merry's Oldsmobile were hand fabricated and fitted into fenders, which had been lengthened about 10in. The headlights used 1955 Buick bumper bullets in the center of the headlight panels, which were backed up with expanded aluminum mesh. The Oldsmobile was finished in Candy Apple Red. Barris Photo Collection

Opposite page
Here I'm grinding on Spence Murray's "Rod and Custom Dream Truck" forming the dual quad eyebrow headlights. I used dual Studebaker pans to make the front grille opening and then formed the quad headlights as I went along, from sheet metal with mesh back plate. We added the pink paint to give some color to the photo. It was estimated that a million and a half people saw the Dream Truck before it was badly wrecked in October 1958. (Kurt McCormick now has the restored Dream Truck in his collection.) Colin Creitz

69

This 1949 Ford sedan became known as the "Curley Flamed Ford." The kid who owned it, "Smiley," worked for me, and he had Jeffries do the entire project, from paint to flames to striping. It turned out really cool.

Opposite page
Bill Carr's "Aztec" was a radical 1955 Chevrolet done by Carr, Bill De Carr, and our shop over a couple of years. It featured 1957 Mercury Turnpike Cruiser headlights, which had been semi-tunnelled, and taillights which were hand-formed in red Lucite by Bob Hirohata. The top was also chopped, with two removable sections and it featured handmade side trim, twin hood scoops, and 1957 Mercury skirts with a scoop. It was featured as the lead photo in the August 1958 Motor Trend story called "The Man Who Changed the Face of Detroit." The feature was about how custom cars and I changed the way Detroit cars looked. Bill Carr had been the 1953 West Virginia Stock Car Champion and loved performance, so he installed a racy Corvette engine. The "Aztec" is shown here with some of its trophies. (The Aztec is now restored and owned by Barry Mazza.)

Above
It's hard to believe, but Art Lehner's Organic Purple roadster was once a 1939 Ford convertible. I liked the style with its nice proportion, but it was also a fun car for both street and show. Known as "The Fadeaway Ford," it was created when the body was sectioned and then channeled over the frame. The body was refabricated with sheet metal into the fadeaway fenders with 1940 Ford headlights and taillights made from 1957 Chevrolet hood scoops and 1953 Chevrolet taillight lenses. It was powered by a chrome-trimmed 348 Chevy with tri-power driving a Corvette transmission. The grille was filled with early Chrysler grille bars and Plymouth bumpers were fitted.

Larry Watson built this 1956 Mercury using a wider outlining. This gave the car an impression of being bronze and gold two-tone. Barris Photo Collection

"George knew how to promote and got us in the West Coast magazines, which was difficult for guys from the Midwest back in the 1950s."

—Alexander Brothers, Custom Car Builders

This 1957 Oldsmobile custom was built at the shop. The Blue Pearl paint with White Pearl outlines followed the chrome and body sculpturing. This neat trick worked out well for this simple mild custom. Barris Photo Collection

The "Wild Kat" Ford F-100 pickup was built for the Srabian brothers, Martin and Morris, from Fresno. We completed it in 1956, beating Detroit to quad headlight styling by two years. It also featured a full custom front and rear with a hand-formed grille opening and tube grille. We finished it in Metallic Rust and then Jeffries added four-tone scallops and a graphic mural on the tailgate. Unfortunately, it never got the magazine or show coverage it deserved, because it was destroyed in the shop fire in 1957.

This traditional 1929 roadster was built for "Whitey" Pollard. I managed to get it featured in the TV Show "Dragnet" with Jack Webb, who is on the left. Notice the Barris crest on the windshield.

We painted the roadster again after the show in lime green with rust flames, and then Pollard took it on the show circuit.

The fire at the Lynwood shop happened during a storm when the power lines banged together and sparks fell on our roof. It was December 7th, 1957, and I lost fourteen cars that night, including Archie Moore's magnesium-bodied Jaguar, Jayne Mansfield's XK-120 Jaguar and the "Wild Kat" pickup. The fire halted at Richard Peters' "Ala Kart." Ironically, he was the only one with the appropriate insurance but didn't need to claim. You can see a burnt Mercury custom we were redoing for Andre and Ron Guidry's chopped 1936 coupe. My insurance company claimed "an act of God."

Dean Jeffries was having dinner across the street and raised the alarm for the fire. He opened the front door of the shop and recovered the Chevrolet belonging to Carol Lewis as the place went up. You can see the remains of the "Wild Kat" Ford pickup in the drive and Archie Moore's custom Jaguar on the left with Jay Johnston and Curley Hurlbert looking it over. The girl I was going with at the time, who became my wife, Shirley Nahas, helped me to get the business back on its feet after the fire. I was ready to give it up; the insurance company never paid off anything.

This 1940 Ford coupe we named "Les Po Po." Bob Crespo had most of the major construction of his coupe done in Northern California by Hal Hutchins before he brought it down to us. All four fenders had effectively been raised by taking an 8in section out of the body and then molding them off flush to the bottom of the body. At the shop we built the hood, frenched in the grille shell, and canted the quad headlights with tubing trim backed up by mesh. The center grille used a tubing outline with a mesh insert and it had three scoops in the hood. The rear matched the front-end styling and nerf bars. It was painted in Skyline Blue Metalflake blended with Candy Blue outlining. Even though it looks like it was chopped, it wasn't, as all the lowering was done in the lower half of the body. (I believe Bob Crespo still has the car.) Barris Photo Collection

Bob McNulty did the design and construction of Bob Moreira's custom Corvette. The design used handformed fins, a 1957 Studebaker Golden Hawk grille, extended fenders with canted Lincoln head-lights, and 1955 Dodge taillights. It was finished in cherry with a silver cove and was later lightly scalloped in silver. It was unusual for a Corvette to have Appleton spots. Barris Photo Collection

Opposite page
This set-up shot of Shirley's "Ultra-Bird" Thunderbird was done for a magazine story with Shirley and me using Kolor Krome products. I built this 1958 T-Bird as a gift for her. I had the headlight housings extended 6in and molded into one piece, a custom grille, and taillights. The 'Bird was painted in thirty coats of Candy Red with white pearl outlining and featured a "T" fin on the top of the rear fenders. I added eighteen louvers down each of the side moldings and had a white, pleated, Carson-look top installed. Another trick to this T-Bird was the hubcaps, which I fitted with red illuminated centers. It won the Motor Life "Car of the Year" award in 1959 after a reader write-in vote. Barris Photo Collection

I saw Richard Greggs' 1950 Ford Tudor pickup during one of my trips to Northern California. He called
it "The Capri." Made from a two-door sedan, the
body was sectioned 5in and the top was chopped a
similar amount to form a cab. Richard did most of
the work, including the custom grille opening, 1957

Chevy front fender tops with light assemblies, and a
tube grille. He also added a 1958 Impala side spear
and "Pell-Pack" lakes pipe guards. This was a very
nice custom including the rear, which used 1954
Pontiac taillights. It was finished off in burgundy with
gold scallops. Barris Photo Collection

This Mandarin Orange metallic 1957 Ford convertible was reminiscent of a Joe Bailon car with plenty of scoops and chromed 1in tubing to make up the bumpers and grille. However, it was built by the owner, Emil Oxen, from Pleasanton, California, who sculptured the side panels, fitted rolled pans, frenched the headlights with open scoops over each light, and fabricated custom side trim. This kind of custom work was a San Francisco Bay Area look, which set it apart from the style we used down south. Barris Photo Collection

This was my 1958 Cadillac de Ville Coupe. It was Candy Apple Red with a Silver Pearl top. I called it the "Kandy Cad." It was nosed, decked, featured a button grille and spotlights, and it was lowered. It was my gift to Shirley when we married.

This 1957 Thunderbird belonged to Dick Jackson who worked for us at the time in Lynwood. The grille was made out of a flat steel strap which was hand-formed with gold plated vertical ribs and a chrome surround. The headlights were formed around 1955 Chevy rims, and it was decked out with lake pipes, twin hood scoops, and was finished in rust with gold scallops and bronze striping by Dean Jeffries. Barris Photo Collection

Jack Preston from Washington state owned this 1953 Studebaker with canted frenched Buick headlights, a grille shell molded around a concave 1954 Kaiser grille, front and rear roll pans. A small 1957 El Dorado Biarritz-type fin is fitted to the rear end above the molded-in Corvette fender sections. It was painted in Candy Apple Red. Barris Photo Collection

The front end of Dawn Smith's 1950 Mercury featured 1957 Chevy headlights, four rows of hood louvers set in a curved pattern, and a modified full-width 1954 Chevy grille. This Northern California car was painted in Avocado Green Metallic with light silver scallops which had white pinstriped edges. Dawn was only 17 years old, as I recall, when we photographed her car. Barris Photo Collection

I shot this 1957 Ranchero belonging to Bob Carter for a magazine story. The Ford was neatly customized by Joe Bailon with quad headlights, side pipes, a 1956 DeSoto grille with lower mesh grilles, and a rolled pan, and it was finished in a bright red. Barris Photo Collection

We customized quite a few motorcycles. This BSA motorcycle featured "ocean wave flames," which looked like repeating flame shapes. It was painted in purple and brown with cream pinstriping. The owner rode it but it was also a show bike. Barris Photo Collection

This 1955 Thunderbird was a clean design, not overly done. Don Tognotti from Sacramento had Corley Anderson and Rick's Body Shop do the restyling. Up front the frenched quad-headlights were set vertically while the grille used chrome cross bars. A 1955 Pontiac split bumper was fitted in with a new rolled pan. Don had 1955 Plymouth taillights fitted into the tips of the stock taillight mounts, with 1958 Impala backup lights in the center. (Don is now the promoter of the Sacramento Autorama and the famous Oakland Roadster Show.) Barris Photo Collection

Indoor custom and hot rod shows were all the rage for quite a while as you can see from the mass of cars packed into this Northern California show. Down south I promoted a lot of indoor shows in the late fifties and early sixties with Shirley's help, eventually doing shows in Pasadena, Glendale, San Diego, Bakersfield, San Bernardino, Santa Barbara, and Ventura. We held them in high school gyms and city auditoriums.

Larry Watson rented a space from us at the Lynwood shop and here he built his famous scalloped 1958 Thunderbird. It featured Kolor Krome bumpers and fully shaved bodywork with electric doors. The lowering job was achieved with chopped and shrunken coils, while the body featured color blending and outlining for which Larry has become famous. Barris Photo Collection

Here is Richard Peters with his 1929 Ford roadster pickup, "Ala Kart." It was a thrash to get the truck finished after the 1975 Lynwood shop fire. It had been slightly damaged in the fire, but we went into overdrive to get it done. Toward the end of its construction, we were nearly living at the shop seven days a week. We finished up the body in Pearl White with purple scallops and gold pinstriping. Wilford, our upholstery guy, did the padded top, the bed, the interior, and all the undercarriage trimming.

The "Ala Kart" was built for Richard Peters based on a 1929 roadster Ford pickup. I sketched this truck out and sold Richard the idea. We built it and then showed it on his behalf. The truck had a custom grille shell which was fabricated with quad headlights and dyed plastic rods mounted on chromed mesh backing. We built the body using a rear section cannibalized from a 1927-T and welded to a 1929-A front section. It was painted with thirty coats of imported Swedish Pearl. The body was trimmed out in extruded aluminum panels. We powered it with a 1954 Dodge Hemi running Hilborn injection,

Vertex magneto, and Herbert cam. This truck was named "America's Most Beautiful Roadster" at the Oakland Roadster show in 1958 and 1959. It was the first to win this award twice. We detailed Ala Kart with ribbon scallops on both the top and bottoms of the fenders and then added reversed underbody trims in padded upholstery. (It is being stored in Arizona and the owner apparently hopes to restore it some day. It was recently listed by Rod and Custom as one of the "Top 20 Rods and Customs of All Time.")

This is Tom Pollard with his 1929 Roadster that was used in the "Dragnet" TV show. It was originally painted red, but we repainted it in lime metallic after the show, adding rust flames to the grille shell lights and fenders. It was flathead powered and featured a chopped T windshield and neat streamlined door hinges.

The "Xtura" Thunderbird 1957 belonging to Mitch Nagao was built in our shop. It featured molded 1953 Studebaker pans which formed the rear grille opening, twin front and rear grilles, flared wheel openings, electric doors, a chrome supercharged engine, chrome reverse wheels, and roof scoops. We finished it in Wild Cherry with Jeffries adding Translucent Platinum Pearl scallops and pinstriping.

Dave Cunningham's 1940 Ford "Li'l Beauty" went through several generations of development. Dave did the sectioning and body channeling with the help of Hutchin's Body Shop, but about 80 percent of the finishing work was done at our shop. We fabricated Pontiac nerf bars and mounted 1941 Studebaker taillights while the fenders were flared and molded in to form coves behind each wheel. The headlights came from a 1957 Lincoln with Lucas lenses. It was painted by Junior in Candy Apple Red with White Pearl scallops. (It is now restored and owned by Dick Falk from Concord, California). Barris Photo Collection

"The Cherry" was owned by Harry Hoskins from Maricopa, California. The 1955 Chevy was built at the shop in Lynwood with a 2 1/2in chop. We molded the grille shell and front fenders, peaked the hood, and lengthened the rear fenders to hold the 1956 Lincoln taillights. The rear bumper features a Pontiac license plate guard. We also painted the Chevy in Candy Cherry and installed a 1956 Corvette grille and 1955 Dodge side trim. This was such a good looking car, it's surprising no one has duplicated it!

The movie Hot Car Girl with Richard Bakalyan and June Kenney featured Frank Monteleone's 1956 Ford convertible. The movie poster called the convertible "Hell on Wheels," but the Ford was only a simple 1956 custom convertible painted in bronze and gold with one of our Continental spares, full-length 1957 Mercury skirts, and the Barris Accessories exhaust system, which came through the bumper.

Here's a photo of the poster from the Allied Artists movie Hot Car Girl, which featured Frank Monteleone's 1956 Ford. The poster is from Ron Main's collection.

Jim Seaton from Santa Maria, California, had us re-work his 1955 Chevrolet. The body featured dual headlights, side pipes, and shaved factory trim. We made the trim from double-molded Dodge side trims, with gold Mylar inserts, and added the custom grille out of mesh and bullets. The taillights were hand-formed plastic with the rear wheel opening framed in tubing to conform with the side trim. Jim also added Kolor Krome trim on the hubcaps, and we painted it in White Pearl with red scallops. (It is now part of the McCormick Collection in St. Louis.) Barris Photo Collection

Jim Doyle from San Jose, California, had Bailon in Hayward, California, build this radical 1952 Mercury convertible custom. The front had a full custom nose treatment and revised rear bodywork with twin Packard taillights. Bailon channeled it 7in and ex-tended the front fenders 9in, tunnelled the head-lights, and then molded scoops into the rear quarter panels. Bailon finished it off with his signature Candy Apple Red paint highlighted with gold scallops. Bar-ris Photo Collection

This 1957 Chevy was built by Bob McNulty for Lau-ralee Dobbel from Hayward, California. Her Chevro-let was shaved with frenched scoops on the hood, quad-headlights, Corvette grille, and a reshaped side panel with a new insert to match the fender shape. As I recall, it was beautifully painted in Frost-ed Turquoise with silver grey scallops. Barris Photo Collection

Bill Hines' "The Bat" was a futuristic 1951 Ford. Bill worked for me at the shop for about a year and later sub-contracted for me when I got busy. Bill built the Ford in Lincoln Park, Michigan, before he moved out to California. The Ford featured a 4 1/2in chop with hand-formed fins and unusual scalloping, which ran the full length of the coupe. Bill reworked his own spindle supports, as I recall, to drastically lower it. Barris Photo Collection

The kustom grille on this 1955 Chevy showed off our new bullet grille kits and our "Kolor Krome" products for a magazine story. We molded off the grille opening and took a section of mesh and set it off with chrome bullets, which we'd treated with Kolor Krome. This formed the grille. We sprayed Kolor Krome on the hubcaps and outlined the Mystic Bronze paint in silver. It looked pretty wild for a few simple tricks.

The "Marquis" was a 1956 Ford hardtop built by Bill Cushenberry in Monterey, California, for Gene Boucher. Bill came up with some radical designs that were amazing. He spent a couple of years working on this car, I recall. The work included sectioning the body 6in, adding modified 1959 Buick rear fenders and frenching in a set of canted, quad Lucas headlights with a matching bullet bumperette. Bill also sculptured the side moldings and the offset peak running down the hood. He finished it in Candy Apple Gold, and it was a super piece of work. Barris Photo Collection

Opposite page
I liked this 1954 Ford Victoria painted in Cadillac El Dorado Green that belonged to Gary Steinmetz from Gilroy, California. Waldon Hogue had done the custom body and paintwork. The front end featured a modified Ford grille, 1955 Chevy headlight eyebrows, and a hood which was peaked and flared into the grille opening. At the rear the Ford featured 1957 Studebaker Hawk fins with 1957 Mercury Turnpike skirts, Pontiac taillights, and a 1958 Mercury hood trim. Waldon had also extended the side body impression and frenched it into the panel. Barris Photo Collection

"If it wasn't for George, custom cars would have never have gotten so big."

—Bill Hines, Custom Car Builder

This 1958 T-Bird was built by Dick Jackson for Cal Wiekamp at the Lynwood shop. The hoods over the headlights were extended 3in, all the trim was shaved, and a full solenoid system was installed for the doors and trunk. The 'Bird was finished in Pearl Blue with Pearl White outlines, and it was one of the late-fifties trendsetting looks. The taillights were from a 1958 Lincoln mounted on a background covered with "glitter." This gave the lights an interesting lighting effect. The grille was built from mesh with "teeth" from a 1954 Corvette grille. Dick got the 'Bird down on the ground with cut coils up front and a C'd frame at the rear. Cal finished it off with a new interior, redone over at Pacific Custom Interiors in Bellflower. Barris Photo Collection

It's surprising how many Corvettes were customized. This 1958 Corvette was owned by Robert Guadagno and was restyled at Bertolucci's Custom Shop in Sacramento, California. The side coves have been filled, apart from one small section, while the nose is all new with an interesting headlight treatment. It was quite an eye-opener with its curved tube grille and slippery lines. Bertolucci was a fine craftsman whom I remember from my days in Sacramento. Barris Photo Collection

Here I'm posing for a Kolor Krome story with some hubcaps in front of our building. Kolor Krome was a transparent painting system which allowed us to add color to chrome surfaces. We also sold colored glitter flakes to which you could add some sparkle. We sold a lot of these rattle cans.

99

Richard "Korky" Korkes came out from New Jersey to work for me after he finished this car. It was built out of a 1954 Ford at Korkes' Custom Shop in Whippany, New Jersey. Korky created the front end using a set of DeSoto and Mercury bumpers set into a custom front end with frenched 1958 Ford headlights. He also fabricated the rear fenders from 1957 Lincoln quarter panels, and the top was made into two pieces with the center removable. The rear treatment was different with its deeply V'd center, custom tube bumpers, and rear grille. Richard was a good bodyman and not too bad with a spray gun either. Barris Photo Collection

This 1959 Chevy Impala hardtop was done by Dick Jackson for Jimmy Cirovello. He outlined and color blended it from dark to light in Candy Royal Blue over a light blue underbase. Barris Photo Collection

Jimmy Cirovello's 1959 Chevy Impala was shot for one of my stories on custom Impalas. It featured a light blue base coat with wild blue fadeaway scallops. The taillights were made as a custom insert using a red plastic Lucite panel with cut-down 1959 Cadillac bullets mounted so their size diminished across the four lenses. They were interspaced with small chrome bullets. Barris Photo Collection

This 1958 Chevy Impala Convertible was brought out to us from Boston. It belonged to Joe Previte and became known as "The Kandy Kart." This was a mild custom done with a chopped windshield, tube bar grille, 1959 Cadillac taillights, chrome reverse wheels, and Candy Red paint. Barris Photo Collection

We did this car twice. In this form it was known the "Modern Grecian," and was one of our most radical four-door customs. The customer wanted something wild for shows built out of his 1948 Studebak-er, so we sectioned, chopped, and channeled it, canted and frenched the headlights, and then covered them with frosted covers. It was painted in Wild Lemon Pearl with Green Pearl side spear.

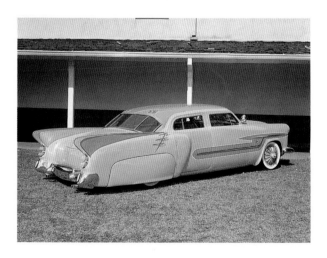

The "Modern Grecian" had a low silhouette hood and featured a floating grille with custom bumpers and our own cast aluminum hub caps.

The Alexander Brothers built this 1958 Ford convertible at their shop on Littlefield in Detroit for Tom Biles from Tonawanda, New York. It featured a white top, tunneled headlights, frenched side pipes, white plastic lense covers, and lowered suspension.

Mike and Larry were fine craftsmen. Their ideas always enhanced the design of the vehicle and every change had a reason; nothing was just stuck on to produce a change. Barris Photo Collection

I photographed this 1955 Chevy in Northern California for a magazine feature. It was built by the owner, Gordon Burnham from Pleasanton, California, and followed the "V-look" that Joe Bailon used. The front bumper was V'd with a matching tune grille and peak off the center of the hood. It was finished in Purple Pearl with radiused wheel openings and chrome reversed wheels. It also had interesting side pipes, which came off the upper part of the front fenders, huge frenched rear license plate mounted in the trunk lid, and 1954 Lincoln taillights with white Lucite ribs. Burnham was a member of Satan's Angels Car Club, as I recall. Barris Photo Collection

Arnie Amoral's 1958 Buick was typical of the mild customs from northern California. It was painted in rust with gold scallops and customized by Gordon Robello of Hayward, California, using a simple custom tube grille, lowered suspension, and chrome reversed wheels. Barris Photo Collection

This purple 1925 T coupe was known as the "Buzz Bomb" after the name of its owner, Buzz Sawyer, from Watsonville, California. Buzz chopped and channeled it over 1932 rails and set it up to run with a heavily chromed full-race 1951 Oldsmobile up front. It also featured wild exhaust headers and a chromed suicide front end, a chopped 1933 DeSoto grille shell, and slicks. It was an eye-catcher and won many trophies for Sawyer. The custom grille shell gave it a new style, and being a 1925 coupe mounted on deuce rails gave it a little more character. Barris Photo Collection

I created this series of trading cards showing the work of custom, hot rod, and race car builders. It sold well and is considered a valuable collectors' set these days. You can see the "Les Po Po" coupe, "Xtura Thunderbird," "Curled Flame" 1950 Ford, "LeMans Cadillac," and the "Li'l Beauty" 1940 Ford.

I wrote these pocket books for "Pete" Petersen's Hot Rod magazine. This collection is mostly "How To's" for detailing customs.

In the late fifties and early sixties I became involved in record album covers and these have become collectors' pieces. "Ala Kart," Li'l Beauty, the Chrisman "Dobie Gillis" streamlined coupe, Sam's "El Capitola," and Chuck Krikorian's Oakland-winning "Emperor" roadster appeared on the covers. We even pro-

duced our own record, called "Kustom City, USA." The Beach Boys' "Little Deuce Coupe" cover featured Clarence Catallo's 1932 coupe, built by the Alexander Brothers. It was then chopped at my shop and painted Oriental Blue and pearl by Junior.

In 1960 we built the "Emperor" for Chuck Krikorian as an Oakland Roadster Show entry. Richard Peters, Chuck's brother-in-law, had won in 1958 and 1959 with his "Ala Kart," so we spent a lot of time making the Emperor just as nice with a hand-formed grille, deck lid, and rear pan to fit the taillights, which were surrounded by a miniature version of the new grille up front. Chuck wanted a fendered rod, so we did the fenders very small with tapered fins. Peters did not compete with his Ala Kart at Oakland in 1960 to give Chuck a chance to win with the Emperor.

Opposite page
In either 1959 or 1960 Joe Burgasser brought in his 1959 Chevy for custom work. It was known as the "The Extasy" after we reworked the Chevy using its bodystyling to create a molded, swooping taillight tunnel, which matched the fender line. It had a mesh insert behind the taillights and for the center of the trunk lid trim we made a chrome insert. The Chevy was painted in Danube Blue Pearl. Barris Photo Collection

The chassis of the "Emperor" was fully detailed and completely chromed. The Cadillac motor was also heavily chromed and featured a white block, Vertex magneto, and half a dozen Stromberg carburetors.

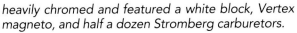

This is Chuck Krikorian with the "Emperor" before it went to its first show. It was painted in cerise with Diamond Dust Pearl lacquer with Tommy the Greek pinstriping. The body was channeled 8in over a 1931 Ford frame, which was "Z'ed," boxed, and chromed, and then fitted with a Halibrand Quick-Change. (This 1960 Oakland winner now belongs to Blackie Gejeian in Fresno.)

Opposite page
Here's the Barris shop at 11054 Atlantic Boulevard, Lynwood, California. You can see Jim Seaton's Chevy, Bob Crespo's 1940 Ford, and Dick Jackson's Thunderbird in the background along with Norm Wesp's 1959 Chevy on the right and a customer's four-door Chevy in the driveway. Wilford Manuel, our upholsterer, is standing with a customer. On Atlantic Boulevard we had four stalls on the right and two spray booths on the left. The neighbors on the left side weren't very happy with us because we worked nights and there was always traffic coming and going. Barris Photo Collection

Spence Murray's Rod and Custom Dream Truck went through a few more mutations before it was painted like this a second time. Five or six different custom builders all added their own little touches to the 1954 Chevy pickup between 1954 and 1958, when it was severely damaged in a towing accident. The truck was used for many magazine stories including ones on the grille, headlights, and the roof scoop conversions we did. (It is now part of the Kurt McCormick collection.)

"I owe everything to George for giving me the opportunity to learn the skills I practice today. He taught me so much in the beginning..."

—Junior, Painter to the Stars

Opposite page
Jerry Anolik's 1955 T-Bird ran a blown Cadillac engine. Jerry was a great kid, and his car was exciting and fun to see. The guys used to rib him about the front end, which was customized after the car was wrecked. Its wildly sculptured nose features four headlights and a bullet grille, while the rear end was treated to 1959 Buick taillights and an exotic-looking louvered and rolled pan. It ran fairly wild, too. Jerry managed 109mph in the quarter with the 'Bird. Barris Photo Collection

Above and lower right
The "El Capitola" was a 1957 Chevrolet built in Carmichael, California, by Sam. He did an extensive amount of custom work to the car, including a unique chop and front end with 96in long 1957 Lincoln fins. It was painted at the Lynwood shop in *Fuschia and Pearl White. The interior featured swiveling seats and a TV in the back seat. Sam built it for Don Fletcher, but it was later sold to Virgil Brinkman. It won the "Full Custom Elegance Award" at the Oakland Roadster Show in 1960. The hubcaps were our own cast-aluminum products.*

"Barris made Detroit stop and look as he dragged the custom car industry into existence."

—Don Tognotti, Show Promoter

Opposite page
Jerry Yatch from Detroit had Bill Hines rework his 1959 Impala hardtop into the "Xcidian." The customizing was carefully worked into the form of the car, but the fenders and fins made it a challenge to form the taillights into a stylish look. Other details included frenched Buick bumpers, frenched license plate, 1953 Chevrolet grille, and molded side pipes with molded hood. Bill finished it off in Candy Apple Red, and there was even a trunk lock insert which replaced the keyhole with a plastic insert inscribed "Xcidian."

Norman Wesp brought his 1959 Chevy Impala from Minnesota to our shop. We added a 1954 Chevy grille center bar with twenty-one vertical teeth, took the scoops out of the hood, added custom 1957 DeSoto station wagon taillights, and painted it in Kandy Red.

Norman Wesp's 1954 Chevy grille looked so neat in the front of his 1959 Chevy when it was all finished. Barris Photo Collection

This 1959 Oldsmobile was a mild custom done for Clay Crowe in Candy Red outlined with White Pearl. It had six headlights with a mass of small chrome bullets over a stock grille and matching rear end bul- let treatment. This part of the job was by Karl Krumme over at Kustoms Inc. in L.A. It also had Dodge Lancer hubcaps treated with Kolor Krome. Barris Photo Collection

I photographed this Candy Apple Red 1958 Edsel built by Rocky's Custom Shop in Modesto, California. It was customized with fine tube grilles, shaved trim, Appletons, white outlining, and lakes pipes. Using an Edsel was most unusual, but it looked neat. Barris Photo Collection

We built the "XPAK 400" in 1959, and it's seen here at the New York World's Fair in 1960. The aluminum body was hand-formed by Jack Sutton from half-hard aluminum. Once it was finished, it won a "Custom Shop Achievement Award" and the "Experimental Class" award on the show circuit. It was functional, floating on a cushion of air, and could be flown by remote control. At first we built it with a gas engine but converted it to electric for demonstrations at the World's Fair. The XPAK was done in red, white, and blue Metalflake with silver trim and featured neon taillights and fluorescent headlights. (It was stored in a hanger at Van Nuys airport, but the owner of the hanger died, and it disappeared.)

This 1952 Chevy was built in New Jersey by the owner, Richard Zadroga. It featured Candy Tangerine paint, Cadillac hubcaps, peaked quad-headlights, rounded corners on the hood, and a doubled-bladed 1957 floating Corvette grille. Richard also added four directional lights using 1959 Cadillac taillights with the red lenses removed. Barris Photo Collection

The "Blue Danube" Buick was featured on the cover of Trend Publishing's Restyle Your Car magazine and in the TV show "Twilight Zone." It was owned by Lyle Lake, who had moved out from Florida and worked for me. The top was chopped 3in in front, but this tapered to 6in at the rear. Side trim was fitted to the body line and wrapped down under the body crease and along the rear fender. It had Kolor Krome hubcaps with 1954 Mercury taillights that were turned upside down and frenched. Barris Photo Collection

The nose of Lyle Lake's "Blue Danube" Buick featured a Barris frenched eyebrow headlight accessory kit. We pressed these out of metal so that it could be welded onto the top edge of the fender. This meant that the original headlights were retained, and a simple custom touch resulted. Lyle also added modified Cadillac bumpers with a gold door-pull mesh grille. Barris Photo Collection

This 1956 T-Bird was built by Joe Ortiz from Hayward, California, for Jimmy Giminez. The nose was heavily sculptured with cutaway fenders and canted 1958 Edsel quad-headlights, double grilles, chopped windshield, peaked scoops above the headlights, and a bumper with a frenched license plate. The rear was reworked with new fins, and the two headrests were created out of headlight buckets. Jerry Sahagon created the interior in matching Teal and White Frieze fabric around handmade tube-framed bucket seats. This was high-tech back then, and it proved to be a big hit on the show circuit. Barris Photo Collection

Opposite page
Joe Ortiz built this 1958 Chevrolet Impala for Chuck Maita from Hayward, California, using a 1959 Buick grille, headlight scoops, Cadillac taillights, side scoops, and bullet hubcaps on chrome reversed wheels. It was painted in Candy Maroon Purple and won several "Semi-Custom" awards. Barris Photo Collection

This 1955 Pontiac Star Chief convertible was an interesting custom done by Bailon for Dave Bennion. Little major surgery was done to this car, but the custom effect was amazing. It retained the factory scoops over the extended and frenched headlights and also used the cut-away factory wheel openings to highlight the combination of colors. Bennion put 105 louvers in the hood and added scallops, Tommy the Greek added the pinstriping, and it all blended into this wild-looking custom. Barris Photo Collection

The rear end of Dave Bennion's 1955 Pontiac was simple but tidy with handmade 1958 Cadillac-style fins and custom round taillights with an eyebrow peak. Barris Photo Collection

I saw "Miss Orchid," a 1950 Cadillac four-door cus-tom, at a show. It belonged to Don Yee from San Jose, who had it nosed and decked with frenched 1955 headlights with a huge scoop in the rear doors while the front was done out with a modified 1953 Chevy grille insert. The rear end had 1956 Lincoln taillights set into 1952 Cad fenders, and it was paint-ed in purple with white impressions around the trim and body moldings. Barris Photo Collection

Bob Whitehead built this unique 1957 Ford Ranchero with custom roll pans and a horizontal tube grille. Small scoops were mounted on each side of the front fenders with a dual exhaust exiting the rocker ahead of the rear wheels. It featured a louvered tailgate and fully customed rear taillights, which used 1959 Cadillac lenses. Gene Winfield painted it purple with fadeaway blues that were blended in different tones. Barris Photo Collection

Mick Tully owned this 1954 Chevrolet Bel Air, which became known as the "Lime Golden Galleon" because of its lime metallic paint. The hood was nosed with rounded corners and molded with a peak. The grille was fabricated using an oval shell with horizontal bars, eyebrow frenched headlights, and a 1957 Chevrolet bumper. The rear end was finished off with 1956 Buick taillights. Barris Photo Collection

Opposite page
The June 1956 Motor Life featured a pair of custom Fords we were finishing. Sam is hammering in the right rear and I'm up front.

Dean Jeffries' custom Porsche Carrera coupe was partly built at the shop using Lucas headlights, which were tunneled into the fenders. The front and back were rolled and it was finished in Platinum Pearl. It was a show stopper for its time and "Jeff" received a lot of attention with many magazine stories and show wins. Barris Photo Collection

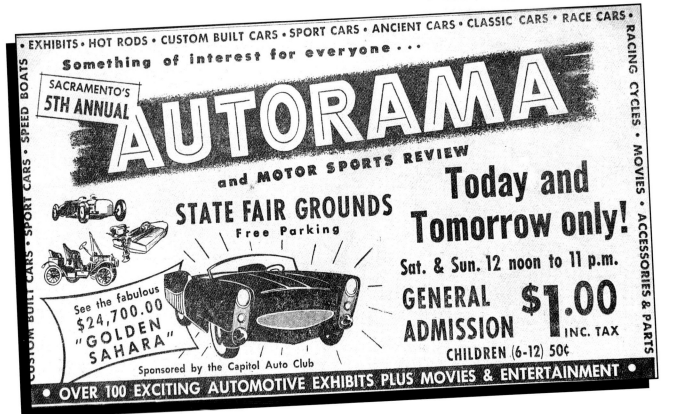

George Barris, 1994.

This is a label from one of my 1-quart Barris Kandy Kolors cans. It listed preparation details to be done before painting and information on how to get the best results.

Index